'SMOKE IN YOUR HEAD'

**25 YEARS OF THE
KINGSTON UPON HULL AUXILIARY FIRE SERVICE
ASSOCIATION**

AND ITS OPERATIONAL UNITS

**HUMBERSIDE VOLUNTARY FIRE SERVICE
PAULL AIRFIELD AUXILIARY FIRE SECTION
AND THE
HUMBERSIDE AUXILIARY EMERGENCY SERVICE**

by

HOWARD BAKER

**HUTTON PRESS
1995**

Published by

The Hutton Press Ltd.,
130 Canada Drive, Cherry Burton,
Beverley, East Yorkshire, HU17 7SB.

Copyright © 1995

ISBN 1 872167 77 2

Printed by
Burstwick Print & Publicity Services,
13a, Anlaby Road, Hull, HU1 2PJ.

CONTENTS

This book is dedicated to...

All who've ever been turned out,
By siren, bell or urgent shout,
Clapped on their brow a helm of brass,
Or steel or cork or fibreglass,
Rode, with excitement and with dread,
In pump of grey or green or red,
To rediscover just how wet,
It's possible for a man to get
And how much mud the world contains,
And what it's like to smell like drains,
How rubber boots are lined with lead,
And helmets built to squeeze your head
How tunics weigh like suits of armour,
And leggings form a twin-limbed sauna
To demonstrate how you can be,
Frozen and boiled simultaneously.
How sweat and strain make you feel faint,
And show you just how fit you ain't!
While locker doors, and gear within,
Will do their best to slice your skin,
And prove how fluent you've become,
At language that would shock your mum,
This tale's for you, though slightly wacky,
And also for Sue and Dave and Jacky.

INTRODUCTION

The Auxiliary Fire Service was disbanded, across Britain, on the 1st April 1968. During the following summer, when it appeared that all trace of the organisation must inevitably vanish, several former members of the Kingston upon Hull brigade decided to pool the photographs and documents in their possession, with a view to establishing as complete a record as possible of the city's AFS. A large amount of material was gathered, some dating back to 1938, and a scrapbook cum-brigade history was created covering the years from formation to disbandment. Subsequently additional volumes were added to cover the activities of the Kingston upon Hull Auxiliary Fire Service Association, which came into being immediately after the disbandment, and to record the adventures of its various operational units: the Humberside Voluntary Fire Service, the Paull Airfield Auxiliary Fire Section and the Humberside Auxiliary Emergency Service.

The information presented in this book is drawn largely from these volumes, and from the personal recollection of those involved, including myself. Having joined the Auxiliary Fire Service in 1964 - following the path previously travelled by both my parents during the war years - I remained with the subsequent Association and served with the various operational units. During the Eighties I used the experience so gained to write two novels about volunteer emergency workers, yet this true account is stranger than either of my fictions. It could be regarded as a story of determined individuals striving to achieve an admirable goal, or it might be seen as portraying a group of amiable eccentrics fighting for a lost cause. I leave the reader to decide.

Over the years many organisations and individuals have supported the Association, in ways ranging from the donation of equipment to the provision of technical expertise. The list is too long to be reproduced in full but particular thanks are due to J.H. Fenner, Reckitt & Colman, BP Chemicals, Humberside County Emergency Planning Service, Mr. Terry Rawson of Sproatley Air Park and Mr. Ron Ducker. Our sincere thanks go to all who have helped us in our endeavours. Finally, too, special tribute must be made to the Association's President, Mr. Norman Murden, in recognition of his dedicated service to the association through its 25 year history.

SMOKE IN YOUR HEADS

Come all you young firemen and listen to me,
All you who go in when the others just flee,
So gay and so carefree with danger you flirt
And get nicotine stains on the tail of your shirt.

You rise with the siren, at top speed you dress,
To go forth and rescue fair maids in distress,
But fair maids have told me, perhaps it is true,
That they weren't in distress till they met up with you.

We went to the bank just to ask for a loan,
We said who we were, how we're all on our own,
"Me name's craft not daft!'" said the man, with a frown,
"Why, your engines blow up and your garage blows down!'"

So listen young fireman, and heed what I say,
You're all raving mad for you work without pay,
You sweat and you strain and curse quite a bit,
And when it's all over you're covered in... glory.

And you don't have the gumption, of that there's no doubt,
To depart from the party when the water runs out, While you risk your necks others lie in their beds,
For you've fire in your hearts but you've smoke in your heads!

THE AUXILIARY FIRE SERVICE - 1938-1968

In July 1938 the government launched Britain's first air raid precautions scheme, which required local authorities to recruit volunteers to assist the professional emergency services in the the event of war. The Auxiliary Fire Service was one element of this scheme, and it attracted volunteers from all walks of life.

The horrors of air attack had already been demonstrated in Spain and Abyssinia and many of those who joined the AFS at that time did so in the belief that the skies above Britain would soon grow black with bombers - a situation chillingly depicted in the film version of H.G. Wells' novel "Things To Come", which was showing in the cinemas at that time. What they did not expect was to fall victim to the hostility of their own side, but such was to be their lot. As the Phoney War dragged on the public took to reviling AFS personnel as cowardly call-up dodgers, while the professional firemen derided them as useless amateurs. The presence of women in the AFS ranks also caused resentment, the Fire Brigade having previously been an all-male preserve. Soon the stigma of being in the AFS grew so onerous that large numbers of recruits left to join the armed forces - so many, in fact, that the newly-established ARP system began to weaken within months of its creation and the authorities were forced to forbid further resignations.

Then came the Blitz, and suddenly the public saw their supposed call-up dodgers through different eyes, while the professionals ceased to judge by uniform insignia. With incendiaries and high explosives raining down the sole measure of a man's worth became his courage and his determination, and with these qualities the AFS crews struggled to overcome their initial lack of experience.

The Kingston upon Hull Fire Brigade and AFS soon found themselves engaged in a savage contest with the enemy, although the city's ordeal was largely concealed by press reports which referred only to 'a north-east coast town'. Particularly devastating raids took place between May 7th and 9th 1941, during which 50 people were killed, over 2,000 dwellings destroyed or damaged and the city centre set ablaze. During that period alone the city's firefighters tackled over 800 fires.

Under the gaze of senior Fire Brigade officers, Auxiliaries establish a 6" pipeline during 'exercise Kingston', which took place on 19th and 20th September 1953. The exercise, which presumed a major fire situation across the Railway Dock, Princes Dock and Humber Dock areas, involved AFS brigades from Hull, York, Bradford, Leeds, and the West, East and North Ridings.

Photograph Hull Daily Mail

Events such as this made clear the vital need for greater co-ordination between Britain's many local authority fire brigades. Accordingly, in July 1941 the nation's brigades were merged and both professionals and AFS became members of the National Fire Service. Only after hostilities ended would it be discovered that Home Secretary Herbert Morrison had, in his haste, failed to take the correct constitutional steps in bringing about this nationalisation and consequently Britain's fire service had been operating illegally for several years.

Early 1950's and an instructor demonstrates a 'deluge set' to a squad of recruits to the newly re-formed Auxiliary Fire-Service. Initially the helmets issued to the AFS were of the World War II 'tin hat' type, but these were subsequently replaced by the NATO- pattern military steel helmet. This latter was not well-suited to the demands of firefighting, and those Auxiliaries who rode with the regular Fire Brigade made a point of acquiring the traditional pattern firefighter's helmet on such occasions.

The passage of the Fire Services Act of 1947 ended the National Fire Service and returned control of the fire brigades to the local authorities. Many of the former AFS personnel, by now experienced firefighters, chose to remain in the Service, joining the ranks of the professionals who had once so derided them. There appeared at that point no reason to re-establish the AFS itself, but within a year it had become apparent that wartime allies did not necessarily make peacetime friends. The Cold War set in with the Berlin blockade and now the sabres that rattled were nuclear ones. Disturbed by the threatening implications Parliament passed the Civil Defence Act of 1948, under which the AFS was re-formed and the other elements of ARP were reconstituted as the Civil Defence Corps.

Auxiliary firemen of Hull's Temple Street depot, pictured in October 1939. Such depots, or 'sub-stations', were established throught the city to accommodate the additional machines and personnel of the AFS. This dispersal system ensured a rapid response to incidents in any part of the city, and served also to limit the number of appliances lost should any one station be hit. A wide variety of buildings, from warehouses to schools, were pressed into service to house the AFS crews and their battleship-grey fire appliances.

Experience had shown that nuclear attack created fire situations of an unprecedented scale and intensity, and accordingly the new AFS was designed on an appropriate scale. For organisational purposes the British Isles were divided into Regions. Within each Region the professional fire brigades were responsible for training sufficient volunteers to create Mobile Columns comprising 694 personnel manning 144 vehicles. The vehicles, supplied through the Home Office, included hose-laying lorries, communications vehicles, Land Rover command cars and transportable water units bearing powered inflatable rafts. The most outstanding item, however, was the Bedford self-propelled pump; a rugged, heavy duty fire appliance that established a reputation for reliability and became known by the affection nickname 'Green Goddess'.

AFS personnel pictured in the lecture room at AFS headquarters during the final days following the announcement of the impending disbandment of the Auxiliary Fire Service & Civil Defence Corps. The headquarters had been home for barely a year.

The volunteers themselves went through a basic 50 hour training course and were then given a uniform comprising firefighting tunic, waterproof leggings and boots, webbing belt with axe and safety line, and a helmet. This latter was the source of much exasperation, being the NATO pattern steel helmet rather than the cork or fibreglass model traditional to the Fire Brigade. The musical crash of colliding steel became a familiar sound wherever AFS men had to work at close quarters, and since the helmet was designed for those who fought with their heads held high rather than those who frequently had to work head-down, it had an infuriating habit of slipping off at inopportune moments. More than one mock-casualty narrowly escaped genuine injury from the falling headgear of a colleague working to release him. In addition to their uniform, AFS personnel received a payment of £10 per year. Not surprisingly, nobody did it for the money.

Her Majesty's Inspector of Fire Services inspects the ladies section of the Hull AFS during the 1967 Home Office Inspection. 'Hull's Fire Belles Are Oh So Pretty' ran one newspaper headline, and the firemen appreciated the fact. Despite a system of separate training nights for men and women, romance blossomed frequently.

Having successfully completed the examination at the end of their 50 hour training course the volunteers were considered operational. They could then participate in the regular exercises held at the Civil Defence Training Colleges at Washington Hall; Chorley, and at Morteton-in-Marsh; the former wartime aerodrome which today houses Britain's Fire Service Technical College. Exercises were also held regularly in major urban areas. 'Exercise Brownroyd', which involved AFS units from twelve cities including Hull, was typical. The 'Exercise Narrative', issued at the time, states:

OBJECTS OF EXERCISE

1 To stimulate interest in the Auxiliary Fire Service by the presence and movement on a large scale of the new type of Emergency Fire Appliances and Equipment, and by publicity in the Press. Also to maintain the interest of those who have already volunteered for part-time service in the various Brigades.

2 To test the laying and operation of 6" Polythene Piping.

3 To test, in part, the City of Bradford Emergency Water Scheme.

4 To test the emergency reception of a large number of reinforcing appliances and men.

5 To test mobilising, Communications and Control arrangements.

6 To test the effects of a concentration of appliances and equipment in a limited area assumed to have been heavily raided and greatly affected by fire.

7 To test the Emergency Meals Organisation and the Women's Voluntary Service.

8 For the Bradford Civil Defence Corps to stage Rescue Incidents within the Fire Zone.

Below: Preparing to get a jet to work aloft... An AFS crew training at North Hull Fire Station in 1965. North Hull Station served as temporary headquarters for the AFS from 1964 until 1966, while the new custom-built headquarters was being constructed adjacent to the then Central Fire Station at Worship Street.

Picture: Hull Daily Mail

SITUATION

There has been an Atomic Strike on the centre of Bradford at 0730 hours on Sunday, 27th June 1954. There is a moderate west wind. Ground Zero is approximately the Town Hall. There is complete devastation of the area within a radius of 4 miles from the Town Hall. Large fires have occurred on the perimeter of the area affected. 7 mobile columns have been mobilised....

Hull's 150-strong AFS set out for such exercises from a headquarters building located directly across the training yard from the city's central fire station in Worship Street. The premises had previously housed Hull's 'Little Theatre', and had only been partially adapted, consequently the new AFS appliances continued to be overlooked by the old upper balcony.

The Hull AFS took a particular pride in its expertise. Partly this stemmed from the city's location, set apart from other major cities, but it also had its roots in the qualities displayed by the old-time Auxiliaries of the Blitz. The newcomers fared well in trying to maintain the old standards. In 1954, at a competition organised in Leeds by the West Riding County Fire Service, a six-man Hull crew gained the Hebden-Royd Trophy by completing a complex firefighting drill in just 44.4 seconds.

But if the brigade's successes were outstanding, so too were its disasters. During one journey to Chorley a despatch rider achieved the unique distinction of reducing an eight vehicle convoy to a three vehicle convoy in far less than 44.4 seconds. As he overtook the convoy, after ushering it through a crossroads, the fire extinguisher fell from his machine, causing the lead driver to brake instinctively. There followed a succession of resounding crashes.... and the self-styled Pride of No. 2 Region were forced to limp into Chorley packed into the only vehicles left serviceable - to the amusement of onlookers from other, lesser, brigades.

The role envisaged for the Auxiliary Fire Service was essentially a wartime one but obviously it was impractical to expect the volunteers to await the coming of war before gaining any fireground experience.. Thus the completion of the 50 hour course also entitled the volunteer to 'book-on' at any fire station and attend incidents with the regular fire brigade. Prospective 'riders' were greeted with varying degrees of enthusiasm by their professional colleagues but a working relationship was achieved overall and Auxiliaries were able to assist at many of Hull's major fires. Those who undertook such duties in the expectation of glamour and high drama were rapidly disillusioned, for many nights could pass without their particular appliance being called upon - although one individual established a much envied record of six turnouts in one shift - three of them coming in such quick succession that the appliance, returning to the station, was twice dispatched again before the crew had time to dismount.

A turnout, of course, did not necessarily mean a fire - and even a fire did not always provide spectacular action. One Auxiliary's strongest recollection from a major dockside warehouse blaze was of being perched on a ladder for several hours, cold and stiff, pouring a jet through a very undramatic, smoking window, while at intervals a voice from the black interior would call: "Here y'are son," and a grimy hand would stretch out with an offering of plump brazil nuts and hazlenuts from the split bags littered amid the wreckage.

There was one night of the year, however, when the Auxiliaries operated as a unit rather than as individuals: November 5th. It was also a night when action was guaranteed, although not necessarily the type of action detailed in the Fire Service Drill Book. The same toughness that had brought the citizens of Hull through the Blitz was displayed annually when the citizens chose to blitz themselves, and during the late Fifties and early Sixties several areas of the city - most notably Hessle Road - achieved Bonfire Night notoriety.

Below: The AFS Transportable Water Unit or 'Bikini', comprised three rafts carried on a transporter, rolled like huge sleeping bags. The rolls were removed by integral crane and prepared for launching by inflation of the side pontoons. A gas-bottle inflation system was incorporated into each raft but economy demanded that inflation be done by foot pump - not a popular task. Each raft was powered by the jet thrust of water from a light portable pump at the rear, and could carry several more pumps on its deck - thereby serving as a floating pumping platform. The Bikini was a popular and effective item, but the slatted deck was notorious for trapping the unwary boot and swallowing smaller items of equipment - anything not tied down vanished swiftly into the depths. The AFS trained frequently at Brandesburton and it has been suggested that the dredging of the Gravel Pits would probably produced sufficient gear to equip a mobile column.

Promptly at 1730 hours the AFS crews would muster in the appliance room, to be detailed to one of the Green Goddesses drawn up in echelon across the yard of Central Fire Station. From 1800 hours onwards all 'Dangerous Bonfire' calls would be handled by 5 man AFS crews, each under the direction of a regular brigade officer. Invariably the first call would arrive within minutes, the chosen crew would race to their appliance and their colleagues would encourage them with calls of "Start limping now!" and "Take no prisoners!"

George 'Ernie' Watkinson directs the crew which gained the Hebden Royd Trophy in 1956. At that time a Sub Officer, Ernie went on to become the most senior officer in the Hull AFS, with rank of Assistant Divisional Officer, and upon the disbandment in 1968 became the first secretary of the Kingston upon Hull AFS Association.

Such advice was hardly exaggerated for the arrival of a fire appliance at a dangerous bonfire usually prompted a fusillade of bricks, bottles and even old bicycle frames. On that night of the year every turnout was a revelation; crews could expect to encounter pavement-to-pavement bonfires sending blazing tar trickling down the gutters and see trees hung with motor tyres, flaming like monstrous Christmas trees. In some areas streets were sealed off against the approaching appliances with planks, dustbins and carpets of broken glass - and on at least one occasion an abandoned bonfire exploded in the firefighters' faces as the heat activated the railway detonators flung into the flames at their approach.

Off Boulevard a Land Rover command car was incapacitated by a brick flung through the windscreen, while a Green Goddess had its door panel neatly drilled by an unknown marksman with an air rifle. On several occasions crews engaged in tackling bonfires were forced to re-deploy to escape the barrage of missiles, and in doing so lost control of their jets just sufficiently to saturate their attackers. On one occasion a group of youths gathered around the rear of a Land Rover and threatened the radio operator. Seeing this, the driver of the Green Goddess behind rolled his vehicle forward, trapped the miscreants by the legs between two sets of bumpers and held them helpless until the arrival of the police.

One crew were fortunate not to lose one of their number when they attended a fire located in a small courtyard. Access was via a narrow alley flanked by high brick walls. Set in one wall was a small door, and behind it - unbeknown to the crew - was a gang of youngsters with ambush in mind. As the first fireman ran his length of hose down the alley, past the door, an arm came out and deftly jammed a lighted Roman candle into the back of his belt. Blinded by the glare of the fire

ahead, and the gloom behind, and hampered by the heavy hose, the man was unable to ascertain exactly what had happened. The truth became clear only when scintillating balls of fire began erupting over his shoulder. He spun; the firework spun too, still roaring and blazing. After several seconds of terrifying confusion a colleague arrived and plucked the firework away, but not before it had burnt a large wedge out of the victim's tunic.

He, at least, was luckier then the fireman whose ear-drum was pierced by the detonation of a firework tucked under his epaullete as he was re-rolling a length of hose. After that incident unfastened epaullettes became standard dress for Bonfire Night.

1954, and a crew inspects the major pump on the first AFS 'Self Propelled Emergency Pump' to be delivered to the city. Subsequently dubbed the 'Green Goddess', the Bedford SSP was powerful and reliable, and although far from beautiful it inspired tremendous affection within the AFS.

Photograph: Hull Daily Mail

It is appropriate that the Hessle Road area, so often the scene of Bonfire Night confrontations, should have become the setting for an AFS legend. It began with a routine turnout to a bonfire which had been lit, rather sacrilegiously, in a tomb in Division Road Cemetery, and which was now igniting the surrounding trees. On arrival two jets were brought into action, and the inevitable barrage of missiles descended. The crew held their ground while stones and lumps of timber ricocheted around the gravestones but immediately the fire was extinguished the officer in charge ordered a hasty retreat to avoid injuries. The retreat proved to be too hasty - as the appliance swung back into the station yard it was realised that one member of the crew was missing. . .

Below: Green Goddesses lined up at Chorley with, on the right, a lorry carrying 6" piping. Such exercises provided the opportunity for crews to replace lost equipment by 'winning' the appropriate item from some rival brigade. However, working in the dark amidst lines of identical vehicles can be tricky, and on one occasion a Hull crew managed to acquire a replacement item - only to discover next morning that another Hull vehicle was now short of it...

He arrived back at Worship Street half an hour later, having sidled unseen from the cemetery and boarded a bus on Hessle Road - in full firefighting kit and clutching the length of hose that he had been rolling behind a gravestone when his appliance departed. Sadly no record remains of the exchange which must surely have taken place when the prodigal was reunited with his crew, but it can well be imagined.

During the early part of the Sixties AFS operations were transferred to North Hull Fire Station on Clough Road, while the Little Theatre was demolished to make way for a custom-built AFS headquarters. This new headquarters was officially opened in January 1966 by the Chief Inspector of Fire Services, in the presence of Hull's Lord Mayor and other civic dignitaries. The celebratory social, on the evening, was marked by a majestically ironic event. The fire-detection system within the building was not set to cope with the heat from the mass of people packed into the first-floor bar and recreation room. Half-way through the evening it activated, setting off a deafening siren and flashing a warning in the control room across the yard. Heavy boots pounded up the stairs and in seconds the revellers were joined by a regular brigade crew in full gear and breathing apparatus. The building was checked, the alarm silenced, and the crew paused for a quick 'half' before ambling back across the yard.

It was an appropriate opening for a building that would echo to the sound of bells and sirens.... for barely another year.

In September 1966 Hull crews were among five thousand AFS personnel from 118 brigades who participated in the largest ever combined exercise. Designated 'Exercise Capital' the event took place at the Royal Victoria and Albert Docks, London, and involved the deployment of ten mobile columns to tackle simulated fire emergencies, using 600 jets and pumping 24,000 gallons of water per minute.

The docks, then about 2 miles long, gave ample room to manoeuvre for the thousand-odd vehicles taking part, while the extensive areas of unpaved railway tracks were useful for simulating rubble conditions. Piping and hose were hauled across this area by hand, and 38 pipe bridges were built to carry water over access roads at double-decker bus height. Equipment brought into play during the exercise included 40 miles of 6" hose, 12 miles of 6" pipe, 25 inflatable dams, 96 heavy and 108 light pumps and 42 inflatable rafts.

'Capital' was an impressive display of firefighting expertise, coordination and resources. It was also a swan song.

By 1967 AFS establishment stood at 12,000 men and women, while the Civil Defence Corps could muster 80,000. Long years of training and exercise work had produced an outstandingly effective system for the protection of the population, and although the past two decades had not brought the nuclear horror once so widely forecast the system had proved its worth at disasters such as the Aberfan landslide and the sinking of the tanker *Torrey Canyon*.

Toward the end of 1967 the government announced its intention to disband both organisations as part of the latest round of defence cuts. The decision was greeted with disbelief. As late as July 1967 the report of the Chief Inspector of Fire Services had concluded with the statement: *Following its review of home defence arrangements the government announced that it would continue to support the fire service in its emergency preparations, including the maintenance of the Auxiliary Fire Service'...*

After the disbelief came anger, and action. Both the AFS and the Civil Defence Corps launched protests. Letters were sent to the Press, MP's were lobbied and a march on Downing Street culminated in the presentation of a massive petition to the Prime Minister, Harold Wilson.

All came to nothing. Despite offers by the combined memberships to forego their annual £10 payments, and to finance their continued operations themselves, the disbandment order was enforced. To each member came a letter....

BUCKINGHAM PALACE

On the occasion of the disbandment of the Civil Defence Corps and the Auxiliary Fire Service I send to all members my appreciation and sincere thanks for the loyal and devoted service they have given this country, some for many years and some in wartime as well as peace.

This is a sad day for you; but your disbandment in no way lessens the value of your services. The spirit of comradeship you have shown, and the example you have set in preparing yourselves for the relief of human suffering and the welfare of your fellow countrymen, have been an inspiration and encouragement to us all.

ELIZABETH R.

The gesture was appreciated, and nobody was inclined to reproach Her Majesty for the decisions of her politicians. But the bitterness went deep, and was perhaps best summed up by a poem which appeared on AFS noticeboards as the final day approached.

EPITAPH

Now, ever so politely, they've explained why you're no good,
You few remaining donors of tears and sweat and blood,
So put aside your axes and let them dull with rust,
Hang your pride up with your helmets and let it gather dust.

Your tough tradition tempered in the fires of the Blitz, In the crackle of incendiaries and the blast of direct hits,
Is strangely out of place today, considered not quite nice,
Your comradeship is suspect, and scorned your sacrifice.

Your exploits are unknown, no-one's televised your toil,
Your badges are illegible for *Torrey Canyon's Roman letters,*
Your floods and your disasters do not stir the heart of Roman,
Your equipment is still stinking from the mud of Aberfan.

Go home and count the death tolls and your lonely vigil keep,
For rescue is expensive and human life is cheap.
Ask not for whom the siren sounds, you're not supposed to care,
The trapped, the burnt, the drowning.... they're no longer your affair.

On April 1st 1968 the Auxiliary Fire Service and Civil Defence Corps ceased to exist. Their fire stations and depots were closed, their vehicles and equipment removed for subsequent disposal. And that should have been that.

THE HVFS SONG

(To the tune of 'Lili Marlene')

H is for old Harold, who tried to see us dead,
V is for the V-sign we gave him back instead,
F is for fightin' on like fools,
And S for stubborn, just like mules,
We are HVFS lads, we've still a job to do

The little men from London took our gear away,
To store it and maintain it, at least that's what they say,
If we'd only known they were flogging it
We'd have pinched a Goddess, bit by bit,
We are HVFS lads we've still a job to do.

We found ourselves an airfield, to tackle something new,
They said: "We need some firemen but you lot will have to do.
All our equipment's up the spout,
So don't just stand there - sort it out!"
You are HVFS lads, you've still a job to do.

Our first engine was Nellie, thirty-one years old,
She started three times out of ten - and not at all when cold,
And when she travelled fast, I swear,
You thought the bleedin'' wheels were square,
We are HVFS lads, we've still a job to do.

We pushed Nellie to standby, and pushed her back again,
We pushed and pulled and towed her, and mostly in the rain,
Charging about in all that mud,
We made Fred Karno's mob look good,
We are HVFS lads, we've still a job to do.

We bought a water tender, the regs had planned to dump,
Everything had been removed, they even took the pump,
We painted and polished till she shone,
And then we glued a new pump on,
We are HVFS lads, we've still a job to do.

We got a rescue tender, you weren't allowed to cough,
For if you did it was enough to make the doors drop off.
Now she's patched up she has got far
More rivets than an armoured car,
We are HVFS lads, we've still a job to do.

Stacks of gear we needed, but we got it all,
If it stands still paint it red, acquire it if its small,
The things you can find if you just seek,
Who cares!... Our case comes up next week,
We are HVFS lads we've still a job to do.

Now H is for the Humber, where we all exist,
V is for the Volunteers, we must be round the twist,
F's for the Fire that burns so bright,
And S for Service, day or night,
We are HVFS lads, we've still a job to do.

Right: The victors with their trophy. Through some oversight the trophy was never recalled for the following year's tournament, and in fact remained with the Hull AFS until disbandment. In 1978 it was officially presented back to the North Yorkshire Fire Brigade, the organisers of the tournament.

HUMBERSIDE VOLUNTARY FIRE SERVICE 1968-1977

It is hard to accept the loss of material things, especially items such as vehicles and equipment that have served well in tough situations, and for which you have developed both an admiration and affection.

It is even harder, however, to be dispossessed of comradeship and a sense of purpose; to be told suddenly that your skills are surplus to requirements, that your dedication and training are no longer required. Across the country many of the former AFS and CDC members managed to make the adjustment and settled into other pastimes. Others sought to establish independent civil defence units, the most successful of which would eventually come together under the title National Voluntary Civil Aid Services, with HRH The Duke of Edinburgh as their patron. Despite such august patronage NVCAS encountered stiff opposition from the Home Office, which refused to grant the organisation a purchase option on the AFS and CDC equipment now scheduled for destruction or disposal overseas. Despite such opposition NVCAS remains in existence to this day, working still to establish volunteer units throughout the country.

It was, perhaps, inevitable that the Kingston upon Hull AFS should produce its own, highly individual response to the disbandment - although in view of the brigade's wartime experience it was rather ironic that this response should involve aircraft. Immediately the disbandment came into force the brigade formed itself into an association, setting out its main object as: 'To maintain and improve skill and knowledge of Fire Service matters, and to offer voluntary service to the community by application of that skill and knowledge'.

Brave words, but it was by no means clear just how this object could be achieved, and as the passing months brought no avenue for action the membership dwindled until just a score of diehards remained. Then, in mid 1969, the Association was approached by the secretary of the Hull Aero Club, which was located on the outskirts of Hull, between the villages of Paull and Thorngumbald. The club had no fire crew, the Association had a redundant one... it was a natural.

It seemed less like a natural when it came to light that the Club's sole item of firefighting equipment was a battered 30-gallon foam tank mounted on the back of an Austin Auxiliary Towing Vehicle dating from World War II. The vehicle soon became known, with something between affection and contempt, as 'Nellie'. 'Nellie' soon became known for her frequent refusal to start when required.

A further revelation concerned the existence of a wide, deep ditch which marked the perimeter of the airfield and left pilots no margin for error on either of the field's two runways, which were arranged in an 'X' configuration. It was a situation more suited to the resident machines of the Bristow Helicopter Company than to the fixed-wing aircraft, most of which were piloted by novices training towards their Private Pilots Licence.

The ditch made its presence felt during the Association's first month at the airfield. Operating for the first time under the command of its newly-appointed officer-in-charge, Peter Metheringham, the crew watched anxiously as light aircraft hurtled across the sky - hardly sparing a glance for the Tiger Moth taxiing sedately along the runway prior to providing a demonstration of wing-walking. Suddenly a gust of wind caught and lifted the aircraft... and it vanished magically as if caught up in some huge conjuring trick. Simultaneously the would-be wing-walker was catapulted out of her harness on the upper wing and described a graceful arc which ended in the ploughed field beyond the ditch.

The crew attempted to turn-out. 'Nellie' refused to start. To allow for this possibility a Land Rover had been borrowed from a local farmer, and this was parked beside 'Nellie'. Determined to put some fast space between himself and the embarrassingly temperamental Austin, the Land Rover driver gave his vehicle full gun - pitching three of his crew off the back in a blasphemous tangle. The three joined forces with 'Nellie's' crew in a frantic push-start attempt and eventually she staggered to the scene, where pilot and wingwalker were recovered with only minor injuries.

The sequence of events was an uninspiring start to the Association's new career - but it would have made superb silent movie footage!

The first standby crew for an air display at Paull Airfield, in the summer of 1969. On the extreme left is Peter Metheringham, the unit's first chief officer. In the background can be seen 'Nellie', the former wartime Auxiliary Towing Vehicle which became notorious for its frequent refusal to start when required. Behind Nellie is the farmer's Land Rover which had been borrowed as support vehicle for this first display- fortunately, as it turned out.

Gradually the members began to get organised, and to adapt to a situation in which everything that needed doing - from establishing crew rotas to acquiring petrol - had to be arranged by them alone; unlike the Central Fire Station days there was no system to arrange such details. Nor was there any higher authority to call upon, other than the Civil Aviation Authority; the sole responsibility of which was to check that the airfield had sufficient firefighting equipment and personnel for its modest number of aircraft movements.

Some of the crew's earliest efforts were notable more for enthusiasm than for efficiency. It was imperative to get 'Nellie' under cover, and an unwanted nissen hut was therefore purchased from a local company. Dismantled from its site in Mason Street this was transported to the airfield, where it was discovered that the crew's failure to mark each section before dismantling had produced a three-dimensional corrugated iron jigsaw puzzle... with no picture to work from. It took three months to rebuild what had been dismantled in a day.

The title 'Kingston upon Hull Auxiliary Fire Service Association' was soon found to be too clumsy, and accordingly 'Humberside Voluntary Fire Service' was adopted for operational purposes, with the Association - under the guidance of an elected committee - continuing to handle matters social, administrative and financial. By now members were paying a small weekly subscription, and in November 1971 the Association was able to purchase a second-hand water tender from the North Yorkshire Fire Authority. The appliance was minus everything including pump but after several months work - including an exhausting trial-and-error saga of pump re-fitting - the vehicle was restored and re-equipped with ex-AFS gear purchased from a second-hand dealer.

On Saturday 19th August 1972 the appliance was deployed for its first operational duty; a flying display stand-by at Burton Constable Hall. At 15.07, On Saturday 19th August 1972 the appliance was deployed in bright sunshine and in full view of the watching crowd, a Nipper aircraft flown by Hull Aero Club Secretary Ken Charles failed to recover from a dive and crashed directly in front of the appliance. The HVFS crew were able to enter the wreckage in a matter of seconds, but the pilot had been killed instantly. A poem written some time afterwards by a member present on that day, catches the atmosphere of that event, and portrays the shock of the crew's first fatal accident.

Left: Paull Airfield's perimeter ditch was the only source of water for firefighting, and neither a reliable nor easily accessible source at that. Accordingly, in 1971, the Association decided to purchase a vehicle capable of carrying its own water. Obtained from the East Riding Fire Brigade, the Association's first water tender cost just £50.

The tail section of the Nipper aircraft which crashed during an air display at Burton Constable Hall on August 19th 1972. Paull Airfield's flying instructor Ken Charles, who was a member of the Barnstormers Flying Circus, lost his life in the accident.

GALA DISPLAY

They gave us gaiety throughout that gala day,
The Floral Dance, in notes of polished brass,
Strauss waltzed a while and sometimes Sousa
marched....
We lay beside our vehicle, on the grass,
Cursed heavy tunics, dreamed of ice-cold beer,
Studied the multi-coloured throng before us,
And bantered with the girls who ventured near.

The tannoy's murmur; echoing, indistinct.
Sunlight on silver, a spark across the sky,
Craned necks and hands upraised against the glare;
We did not watch, we only heard you die.
Sprang up as joyful waves of music
Swelled to fill the eerie silence of the stall,
In a frozen instant glimpsed the stricken splinter,
Claw at the indifferent sky, and fall....

Impact. Stark above the siren's scream,
Trembling through the boots braced to the floor,
A vividness of sight and scent and touch,
Bright helmets and hot oil, the crewcab door
That opened out into another world
Where summer and its carefree games were gone,
And ugliness was all, and carnage reigned,
Yet strangely, distantly, a band played on....

The loss of Ken Charles was keenly felt by the crew, for it had been he who had originally invited them to the airfield. But the incident also brought a definite realisation of the vital nature of an airfield fire crew's role and a determination to fulfil that role as professionally as possible.

Shortly afterwards 'Nellie' finally disintegrated (possibly, as someone remarked, in protest at the arrival of a new water tender). Hull Aero Club replaced her with an Austin Gypsy, and this was soon equipped as a Rapid Intervention Vehicle. At the same time the acquisition of further equipment gave the water tender the capability to deliver 3,000 gallons of foam. This was more than enough to blanket the usual Condor, Cessna and Aztec aircraft, and sufficient to cater for Bristow's Whirlwinds, which journeyed regularly between the airfield and the North Sea oil platforms. As volunteers, the crew were unable to be present at the airfield at all times but developed a routine of training there one night a week and being present during weekends, when most flying training was carried out, and at all 'high-risk' times such as air displays. To cater for the remaining periods the crew trained pilots and ground staff in the use of equipment and established strict emergency procedures. A warning siren was fitted to the roof of the air-traffic control shack, from where it periodically announced that the perimeter ditch had claimed yet another victim...

One such was an attractive young lady from a neighbouring airfield. She landed one Sunday afternoon, misjudged the length of the runway and was still travelling at high speed when she arrived at the end. Attempting to overshoot, she hauled back on the stick. The aircraft's tail slammed into the ground with a crash that could be heard inside the clubhouse and the machine sprang over the ditch and crunched into the deep-ploughed field beyond. Shedding pieces in all directions it lurched over the ruts for about a hundred yards, whereupon the nose-wheel collapsed and the aircraft forward-rolled majestically onto its back, stuck its wheels in the air and expired.

Alerted by the siren the fire crew roared across the newly-constructed emergency bridges in a frenzy of blue lights and two-tone horns and arrived at the scene expecting to discover the worst. Instead they found the young lady hanging upside down in her harness. but otherwise intact. Retrieved from her undignified position she clambered to her feet, eyed the crew with massive disdain and informed them:

"Your stupid runway is too short for my landings!"

Such lines came to be treasured by the crew, who found many of the pilots gifted with an intriguing ability to deny logic in that manner so familiar to vehicle insurance assessors.

"It was a perfect landing!" complained one student, after bouncing his aircraft in like a Mach 2 pogo stick. "Perfect! It's just that the ground moved..."

Neither was the comedy confined to words; the pilots were good at the live-action stuff too. One afternoon the crew responded for a pilot who had noticed a smell of burning in his cockpit. He landed safely, despite the large bird's nest which the crew discovered smouldering gently away under the engine cowling. Another pilot had the unnerving experience of hearing an insistent tapping on his cabin door while cruising at 4,000 feet. He landed hastily, looking pale, but his colour rapidly returned when it was discovered that he had trapped his passenger harness in the cabin door and the buckle was tapping to come in...

The vagaries of the British weather also provided some memorable moments. Even major airports can fall victim to the elements; with a small airfield it is simply no contest. On occasions the wind-speed was such that crew members had to form a double line along the runway and catch the wingtips of the aircraft as they touched down, lest they be blown onto their backs. On occasions, too, the standing water reached such levels that an aircraft touching down would instantly explode into a whirling ball of spray with a wing-tip sticking out at each side.

"My god, it's a flying block of flats" remarked one of the crew when Blackburn Beverley XB 259 appeared over Paull Airfield on Saturday 31st March 1974, and even after touchdown it continued to dominate the landscape. Concern had been expressed regarding the massive aircraft's ability to land in the distance available, but under the control of Sqdn. Ldr. P. Sedgwick, officer commanding the Western Test Centre at RAF Farnborough, XB 259 displayed the characteristics which had made its type famous - it rolled to a halt in just 400 yards.

On one occasion thick fog blew in from the Humber and blanketed the airfield in a matter of minutes, forcing the crew to position the water tender at the end of the runway, all lights blazing, to serve as a beacon for a pilot caught in the sky. For several minutes the crew sat peering into the sky, at which point there loomed from the fog a twin-engined Aztec at a height and heading that could only take it through the vehicle's nearside door. Six crewmen curled up in an instinctive attempt to lower the cab roof, and somehow the aircraft staggered over the obstruction and touched down safely. Later it was rumoured that the next crew to wash the vehicle discovered tyre marks on cab roof...

On 23rd, 24th and 30th of March 1974 HVFS crews stood by for the arrival at Paull Airfield of the last flying Blackburn Beverley Freighter, No. XB 259, which Hull Aero Club had acquired from Farnborough and were hoping to transform into a clubhouse. The three day standby was caused by bad weather conditions which twice forced the postponement of the take-off from Farnborough. The Beverley at last took to the air on Saturday 30th, but with half an hour to go before its arrival Paull Airfield was blanketed by smoke from a large bonfire built by council workmen in the nearby village of Thorngumbald. The water tender was dispatched, the situation explained to the startled workmen and the fire extinguished and the water tender returned in time to see the Beverley touch down safely at 5.32 p.m. Remarkably, by 5.40 thick fog had blanketed the airfield and the crews were called to stand-by for a training aircraft having difficulty locating the field. The pilot eventually landed safely.

Sadly the Beverley never did become a clubhouse - the demands of the Building Regulations proved prohibitive. But at least the fire crew gained something from its presence. It was discovered that the trapdoor in the massive tail, formerly the exit for paratroops, was ideal for practising rescues from heights - a skill that was to become increasingly necessary thanks to peacetime parachutists.

By now Humberside Voluntary Fire Service was well-established as an airfield fire & rescue crew and memories of a former existence as an Auxiliary Fire Service unit were fading, particularly as membership had now been augmented by several newcomers from the flying fraternity.

Then, on the afternoon of Saturday, 1st June 1974, the past came back into focus with a vengeance. At 4.50 p.m. on that afternoon a pipe fractured within the Flixborough Nypro Plant on the South bank of the Humber, and three minutes later escaping chemicals ignited. The resulting explosion was Britain's largest ever in peacetime. 29 people died instantly, over a hundred more were injured. The effects of blast and falling debris - some of which landed ten miles from the explosion centre - destroyed over a hundred homes, while clouds of fumes forced the evacuation of villages on both sides of the river. Under a mile-high column of smoke the emergency services began to battle with a holocaust that would rage out of control for over 24 hours. It was, in fact, the classic scenario for an AFS mobile column.

The Humberside Voluntary Fire Service offered its assistance. but was not used at the scene. Instead its members remained on standby at the airfield throughout the following day, making available the water tender for use by the Authorities on a North Bank almost depleted of regular brigade appliances by the scale of the disaster. It was a day of endlessly checking equipment and periodically slipping into the airfield clubhouse to catch the latest developments on TV. At one point a chartered aircraft flew over the fireground, relaying pictures of the devastation. As the flame fringed tower of smoke filled the TV screen the awed silence in the clubhouse was broken by a crewman's enquiry.

"Jee-zus! Did the Chief really volunteer us for that?"

Left: A Westland Whirlwind lifting off from Paull Airfield for its regular trip to the North Sea oil rigs. At bottom left can be seen the wreckage of this aircraft's predecessor, which ditched in the North Sea and had subsequently to be winched from the sea bed. All those aboard were rescued without injury.

Below: From the ridiculous to the sublime... purchased by the Hull Aero Club, this ex-military Land Rover was restored, equipped and made fully operational by the Association's members over a three month period.

Above: Water tender crew swilling away a fuel spillage. After the days of relying on Nellie, the trailer pump and water from the perimeter ditch, it was reassuring to have a 400 gallon supply constantly on tap, and the acquisition of additional equipment soon enabled the water tender to deliver foam.

Right: As the scope of Paull Airfield's air displays widened, attracting increasing military participation, the Association sought assistance from RAF Leconfield and was provided with training in the handling of ejector seats.

Someone confirmed that this was so.

"I think, mused the speaker, 'that there's a lot to be said for secret ballots..."

But if the Association was allowed to contribute little during the Flixborough disaster it was able to undertake an increasing workload at Paull Airfield. Throughout 1975 the number of aircraft movements increased steadily, and this brought the need for effective co-ordination of emergency operations. A former ambulance was therefore purchased from a disbanding rock group, and the interior rebuilt to enable the vehicle to serve as a mobile control unit. At the same time one of the original stretcher racks was replaced, giving the vehicle a dual function - and leading to a classic bureaucratic encounter.

Fire appliances are exempt from Road Fund Tax, a fact greatly appreciated by the impecunious Association. Exemption was therefore requested for the new control unit, and photographs were supplied to the local taxation office to prove that the vehicle was liveried, beaconed and equipped as befitted a fire appliance.

The stretcher rack proved a stumbling block. Fire appliances were exempt, so too were ambulances - but there was nothing in the books about a vehicle with the attributes of both.

"Why have you re-fitted the stretcher rack?" came the question.

The Chief explained that it would enable casualties to be transported immediately from the rather isolated environs of Paull Airfield and transferred to the responding ambulance en route - thus saving time.

"But what if such a casualty should die before you rendezvous with the incoming ambulance?" asked the official.

The Chief was understandably puzzled but alert enough to point out that no casualty carried by the vehicle could officially be dead - even if death was obvious - since no member of the crew had the authority to declare a person dead. Therefore any corpse would remain alive, technically, until declared otherwise by a doctor.

The official mulled this over for a moment before delivering the sombre warning: "Bear in mind, if you carry someone who's dead you have to have a Goods Licence, otherwise it's a serious matter..."

It took six months and reams of correspondence, but eventually the exemption was granted.

By now Paull Airfield had become the venue for the annual Hull Air Show, which attracted aircraft very different from the resident light trainers. Even if Vulcans and Buccaneers could not land on such short runways their presence overhead presented potential problems. Fortunately the crew's anxieties were appreciated by the Fire Section at nearby RAF Leconfield which obliged with training sessions on crash-rescue techniques, emphasising particularly the special hazards of armaments and ejector seats. RAF Leconfield's help was greatly appreciated. Earlier that year, down South, a would-be rescuer had accidentally activated the explosive release on a crash-landed fighter, and had been taken eighty feet into the air by the ascending canopy. It was one of the many perils not immediately apparent to the uninitiated - and the experience was not not one that anyone on the crew wished to emulate.

Early in January 1974 Hull's Old Town was flooded once more - a regular occurrence in those days before the creation of the tidal barrier. HVFS crews were called in to assist and spent a Sunday trying to return the river to its appointed place. It was a messy, smelly task, but the experience produced one creative masterpiece which was performed with gusto at the next social....

THE MUD SONG

One bright Sunday morning as I lay in bed,
A dreaming of boozing and birds,
A very loud telephone went off near me head,
And I muttered some four-letter words,
But it kept on and on till I crawled out of bed,
And shouted "Whasmarrer?", and here's what it said....
Mud, mud, glorious mud,
Plastered all over like brown sago pud.
Me factory's sinking, or maybe it's shrinking
It's certainly stinking with glorious mud.

So I put on me battle gear, me tunic and cap,
And set off to look at the sight,
Some twit had forgotten to turn off the tap,
So the river'd been filling all night,
But we sang as we worked, till the rafters did ring,
And these I assure you are the words we did sing....
Mud, mud, glorious mud,
You try hard to shift it, but it's no bloody good,
For the damn stuff is gluey, and sticky and gooey
And by hell it's pooey, it's glorious mud.

So we cleaned out the factory, chucking mud near and far,
And started on the tavern next door,
But when we had shovelled a path to the bar,
We collapsed in a heap on the floor,
And as they revived us with tankards of ale,
We sat bolt upright and we started to wail....
Mud, mud, glorious mud,
Remember to call us when you have a flood,
We'll put on our kit for, if there's one thing we're fit for,
It's shovelling ... for it's glorious mud!

The wet weather didn't last, and come the spring there occurred an incident which provided a hint of problems to come. While standing by for routine flying one afternoon the crew suddenly found the runways enveloped in smoke blowing in from the surrounding countryside. Within minutes blue lights winked along the distant perimeter road, and an officer was dispatched in the Gypsy to identify the newcomers and offer any assistance that might be required. It turned out to be the retained fire crew from the nearby village of Preston, who were happy to accept the offer of assistance - and soon the HVFS water tender and crew joined the Preston brigade in tackling a rapidly spreading undergrowth fire. Gradually the blaze was contained, but not before several telegraph poles and several hundred yards of fencing had succumbed. As the blackened crews were making up their gear they heard a policeman wearily admonishing a young farmhand:

In 1974 BP Chemicals presented the Association with this 1950 Rolls/Dennis F2 fire appliance, which had become surplus to the company's requirements. Unfortunately the task of renovation proved too extensive, and efforts to restore the vehicle to operational condition had to be abandoned. Instead it was dismantled into its component materials, and these were then turned into cash. Thus the Association gained its first substantial equipment fund. Not quite the contribution which the vehicle had been intended to make, but an invaluable one all the same.

"You've got to get a grip on your old man and his controlled burning, lad."

"Get a grip on him!" protested the youth. "Hell, the first I knew was when he comes galloping in the kitchen shouting 'Holy Christ, I've set the farm on fire!'...

It was the kind of cry that was to be heard with growing frequency in the coming months. The summer of that year was one of the hottest and driest on record and the incidence of scrub fires and forest fires increased at a rate that took even experienced fire chiefs by surprise and caused Lord Harries of the Home Office to declare: *'Property and life has never been at greater risk. The situation is without parallel in peacetime'*...

By early August the situation was even further without parallel. Massive woodland and forest fires raged throughout the country, destroying entire plantations and forcing the evacuation of scores of villages. For a while the county of Dorset was almost cut off by raging fires, while up on the North Yorkshire Moors hundreds of acres of peatland blazed. Throughout the country the shortage of manpower and equipment became apparent, appeals went out for volunteers, and thus HVFS crews journeyed to the North Yorkshire Moors to help relieve the crews operating there. Some of these had been continuously engaged in the struggle for three weeks, as was apparent from their blackened and begrimed state, and the undefiled smartness of the HVFS newcomers prompted one veteran to greet their arrival with the cry: "Christ, things must be bad - they're sending us tin soldiers now!"

In its initial stages the fire had been awesome in its magnitude - "so big it was exhilarating" as one of the local firemen admitted - and at one point a change in wind direction had forced the firefighters to retreat and caused the loss of one appliance and a quantity of equipment. By now, however, the conflict had become a war of attrition, with the fire sprawling over a vast area rather than leaping high, and the firefighters, dwarfed by the huge smoke column, struggling to block its progress with bulldozed firebreaks.

Left: Following the final demise of 'Nellie', Hull Aero Club purchased an Austin Gypsy which the Association transformed into a Rapid Intervention Vehicle. While lacking the character of its predecessor, the Gypsy could at least be relied upon to roll when required.

Detailed to work on Rosedale Moor, close to the Fyllingdales Early Warning Station, the HVFS crews pitched in, displaying a certain eagerness to get as dirty as possible as quickly as possible. Deployed along a firebreak, one crew promptly experienced a poignant reunion for lumbering over the moor, relaying water to the most hard-pressed points, was an ex-AFS Green Goddess; now painted yellow and dubbed by the North Yorks men as 'Yellow Peril'. It was, in fact, the only vehicle capable of traversing the terrain - the low clearance of the standard fire appliances confined them to the roads.

Supplied with water by the 'Yellow Peril', the firebreak crew set in and trained jets across the firebreak- but soon discovered that moorland firefighting had unusual aspects. Denied lateral movement the fire had begun to burn deep into the peat; deep enough, in fact, to tunnel beneath the firebreak. Periodically spirals of smoke would rise behind the firefighters as the fire began to surface once more, and it was then necessary to re-train the jets hastily in the opposite direction.

Elsewhere a second HVFS crew had been detailed to knock out such 'hot spots', using narrow-bore high pressure jets capable of cutting through the peat. This, they discovered, was the ultimate method for achieving instant dirtiness. Slicing into the peat, the water boiled into steam immediately it reached the burning heart, expanded explosively and threw up geysers of blackened water, ashes and charred peat. Within half an hour the once-tidy crew resembled a company of incinerated scarecrows.

One crew member was detached to assist a local retained fireman in ferrying water from a small stream in a deep valley. Returning through the valley the vehicle ran out of fuel, stranding the pair in a canyon surrounded on three sides by walls of smoke. While the driver radioed for fuel the crewman alighted, stared round at the ominous view and eventually enquired with a massive show of unconcern: 'So what do we do now, then?"

"We declare opening time" announced the driver, imperturbably, leaning back in his seat and opening an equipment locker to reveal assorted cans of ale...

Far from being a relief, the arrival of a staff car and jerrycan was almost disappointing.

The HVFS crews which returned to Hull late that night were unrecognisable as the ones which had set off early that morning. But if they were bedraggled they were also buoyant with the knowledge of a job well done, and of having at least made some contribution to the efforts going on around the country. Shortly afterwards those efforts prevailed with the vital help of the weather.

The drought finally broke, fierce storms lashed the British Isles and with their help the weary firefighters, assisted by troops, succeeded in quelling the fires. Even so, many of the moorland outbreaks continued to smoulder deep into the peat for several months.

The end of the Humberside Voluntary Fire Service era came out of the blue, the following year. It was an end precipitated by an incident which was basically comical but which held unfortunate undertones of the tribulations suffered by the AFS during the Phoney War.

On a glorious Saturday in June the HVFS crews ventured from Paull Airfield to participate in Hull's Lord Mayor's Parade. Appearing last in the order of parade the crew marched while the water tender followed. All went well until they were within a hundred yards of the

A crew line-up prior to the 1977 Air Show at Paull Airfield. In the early operational days the standard firefighter's helmet was black, but white was adopted by the Association to ensure high visibility out on the runways. Initially this caused some bemusement when regular brigade crews were encountered, for in the Fire Service a white helmet signifies a senior officer and thus the Association's crew appeared to comprise all chiefs and no indians. Subsequently the visibility factor became more widely appreciated and yellow was adopted by Britain's Fire Services, whereupon the Association conformed. In the background can be seen the Blackburn Beverley which now resides at the Museum of Army Transport, Beverley.

route's terminus at East Park. There the water tender, having covered four miles at walking speed on a hot day, 'gassed-up' and stalled. The crew marched on, the water tender was re-started quickly enough to re-join them as they entered the park gates, and the hiccup was forgotten.

But not, unfortunately, by everyone.

A member of the public, having seen the vehicle stall, telephoned Fire Brigade Headquarters complaining about the apparent inefficiency of the County's fire appliances. The Chief Fire Officer was understandably upset, and - not so understandably- announced as much in the press; condemning the HVFS personnel as: 'Scruffy, long-haired alleged firemen, wearing quasi-firemen's uniforms and using unofficial fire appliances bearing the name Humberside'.

The Association was dismayed. All of its members had been smartly turned out for the parade, only the ladies on the crew had hair which could be termed long, and as members of the British Fire Services Association - and an airfield fire crew recognised by the Civil Aviation Authority - all were entitled to be in uniform,

The injustice was compounded by the fact that the designation 'Humberside' had been adopted by the Association some two years before the county boundary changes forced the Local Authority to adopt it.

But you can't fight City Hall, and a lengthy dispute could only reflect badly on the Fire Service as a whole. On the evening of Tuesday 23rd August 1977 an Extraordinary Meeting of the Association was held at Paull Airfield to debate the question of replacing the existing operational title with one which could not, in any way, be mistaken for that of the professional fire brigade.

The change was agreed, and the title chosen was 'Paull Airfield Auxiliary Fire Section'.

During the drought summer of 1976 Association members travelled from Paull Airfield to the North Yorkshire Moors to assist in containing a major fire on Rosedale Moor. One of the crews is seen here with the 'Yellow Peril', a 4 x 4 ex-Green Goddess of the North Yorkshire Fire Brigade which proved invaluable for ferrying water across the rough terrain.

THE WILD FIREMAN

(To the tune of The Wild Rover)

I've been on this fire crew for many a day,
And me knees are all wobbly, me hair's turning grey.
I'm half me time praying, and holding me breath.
Cos these bloody toy aircraft they scare me to death.

I've seen 'em with bent props in need of repair,
And laid on their backs with their wheels in the air
I've peered through the fog at an aircraft unseen
And got tyre marks on me cab roof to show where he's been.

I've towed in a Condor with a tail-wheel collapse, And
I've seen pilot's hung upside down in their straps,
Magnetos and oil caps they've lost while in flight
And I'll swear they just do it to give me a fright.

I've heard aircraft falter, and splutter and cough,
And I've watched 'em plough in when their nose-wheels drop off,
I've seen 'em land sideways and snake all around,
Or just taxi along till they run out of ground.

Now I wouldn't know if the aircraft are bad,
Or the people who fly 'em are all raving mad,
But no more I'll fly and be scared into fits,
I'll just stay on the ground and I'll pick up the bits.

AFS Association Secretary 'Ernie Watkinson presents the British Fire Services Association's Long Service Medal to Peter Methering-ham, the unit's first operational chief officer.

PAULL AIRFIELD AUXILIARY FIRE SECTION 1977-1981

After the Lord Mayor's Parade experience it needed something pretty big to tempt the newly-christened operational section from the security of its airfield perimeter - but Nature duly provided this in January 1978. It came in the form of heavy seas, high tides and 80 mph gales that toppled trees and chimneys, and sent floodwater sweeping into Hull's Old Town area. Responding to a request from a member of the public the crew slipped into the city to undertake flood relief work, and slipped unobtrusively out again when the waters receded. As one member observed: it was ridiculously like trying to operate a resistance group in occupied territory.

Later that year Hull Aero Club purchased a foam tender from British Aerospace at Brough, and the ageing Austin Gypsy was replaced by a Land Rover. The complement of emergency vehicles now comprised a water tender, a control unit, a rapid intervention vehicle and a foam tender; making Paull Airfield one of the best-equipped Category 1 airfields in the country.

It needed to be. The scale of the air display continued to increase, bringing in such famous names as the Red Arrows and the Rothman's Aerobatic Team. The fire crew's anxiety, once focused on jet aircraft, now shifted to their predecessors; aircraft such as the Hurricane and Spitfire of the Battle of Britain Flight, and the last flying Lancaster and Flying Fortress. There was a general trepidation about ever having to tackle an incident involving one of these, for fear of any additional damage which might inadvertently be inflicted on their precious, antique structures.

Another anxiety-producing element was the inevitable display of parachuting. The Army Teams invariably landed on the marker, the freelance teams invariably landed off it - sometimes way off it. Retrieval of parachutists from surrounding fields became so commonplace that it was rumoured that the local farmers were clubbing together to purchase an anti-aircraft gun.

On one occasion the crew found their man hanging in the topmost branches of an oak tree and had to spend so long trying to untangle his canopy that Air Traffic Control instructed the next display aircraft to over-fly the scene and report. Thus, just as the crew began the delicate task of lowering the victim to the ground, there burst over the scene, at zero feet, the sinister bellowing shape of a Messerschmitt 109. The crew kept their nerve, but not so the bullocks which had gathered to watch their efforts. Galloping around in panic they homed in on the nearest alien item - the Land Rover - and began butting it with increasing fervour until scattered by the aircraft's second pass. Getting the parachutist hastily down to ground level the crew bundled him into the vehicle and beat an undignified retreat that was distinctly reminiscent of Dunkirk.

Even when everyone managed to hit the drop zone there could still be problems.. .

"Why has the last man got a red emblem on his jump suit?" enquired a newly-recruited young lady, standing at the door of the control unit and peering through binoculars at a descending stick of parachutists.

"It could mean he's the team leader.'" someone offered.

It didn't. It actually meant that the unfortunate jumper had caught his hand as he sprang from the aircraft, and consequently he was bleeding prodigiously while two of his fingers cruised several thousand feet overhead.

Above: A Static display At the Fenner Gala during the summer of 1977, following the change of name to Paull Airfield Auxiliary Fire Section. By now Association funds had accumulated sufficiently to allow the purchase of a quantity of ex-AFS firefighting hose, a range of modern extinguishers and various specialist items including a Portapower hydraulic rescue set and visored helmets for close-quarter aircraft accident work.

Right: Foam team at work during a gala display in the summer of 1977. With the crew relying for finance solely on the weekly subscriptions of its members, the use of resources such as foam compound had to be tightly restricted. Displays such as this thus combined crowd entertainment and crew training.

Left: The Association gained the permission of Associated British Ports to utilise Alexandra Dock for the testing of their pumps, and such visits provided an excellent opportunity to practice 'branch-ending'.

Below: For the 1978 air show the Association's vehicle line-up was supplemented by a visiting pump-escape operated by a group of enthusiasts from South Shields. During the event some 12,000 spectators were treated to displays from the Red Arrows and the free-fall parachutists of the RAF Falcons, plus such World War II veterans as the Spitfire, Hurricane, Messerschmitt and B-17 Flying Fortress.

Then there was the gentleman whose display routine consisted of jettisoning his chute after it had opened, free-falling for long enough to scare the crowd then opening a second chute. Unfortunately he forgot to mention this to the crew.

"Ooo-eek!"' gasped the crowd, as the first chute whipped unexpectedly away.

"Oh shee-it!"' groaned the crew, transfixed by the sight of strawberry jam arriving in quantity.

The blossoming of the second chute was greeted by the crowd with sighs of relief. The realisation that the incident had been deliberate produced profanities among the crew. Gently the parachutist floated down, acknowledging the enthusiastic applause appropriate to a man who has just slid down the sky at breakneck speed and chanced his luck twice in one jump. That being the case it was ironic that he should stumble at the moment of touchdown, and very unkind of his chest altimeter to jerk upwards, whack him in the mouth and remove his front teeth...

The victim was recovered and tended by three members of the crew. It would have been more but the rest couldn't stand up for laughing.

The rules governing the operation of airfield fire and rescue services are embodied in Civil Aviation Authority Regulation CAP 168, and once a year the CAA Inspector of Fire Services would arrive at Paull Airfield to check that all was up to standard. The check consisted of a day-long inspection of all procedures and resources, followed by an evening exercise to test the response and abilities of the personnel.

The crew never failed to acquit themselves well on these occasions but always, too, the tension of working

under close scrutiny led to errors of the more-haste-less-speed variety. On one occasion the crew were required to recover a casualty from a field beyond the perimeter ditch, without using the emergency bridges. The ditch was duly bridged with a ladder, covered with jack plates and timbers to form a walkway, and safely crossed. On the return journey, however, the crew - now transporting a mock-casualty roped to a stretcher - ran into trouble. Half way across the ditch one of the leading men put his weight on a timber which broke, tilted and caught the following man squarely under the knee, plunging his leg down into the space between the rungs. Three men fought to retain their balance while the fourth struggled to extricate his leg, and between them, on a wildly tilted stretcher, the helpless casualty peered down into the depth below - uncomfortably aware that he would shortly be heading that way if they didn't get themselves sorted out. Eventually stability was restored, the crossing completed and the casualty delivered unharmed - much to the credit of the unfortunate crewman who now had a badly bruised leg and was therefore better qualified for the stretcher than the casualty he was carrying.

The 1979 inspection produced a similar hiccup that brought tears to the eyes of a Hull Aero Club pilot who had recklessly volunteered to serve as a casualty at a location known only to the CAA inspector.

The stage was set, the siren screamed and the vehicles turned out to Air Traffic Control for details of the incident. It proved to be an explosion in the airfield's newly-constructed aircraft hangar; a building of curved roof construction similar to a nissen hut. Working by torchlight and floodlight the crew tackled the situation but at first were unable to locate one person known to have been present at the time of the explosion. Then someone outside the building spotted a figure sprawled high on the roof...

A

D

B

C

The performers at Paull Airfteld's air displays spanned a vast era in aeronautics, ranging from the aircraft of World War II to the aircraft of the war which never happened.

A. *Spitfire of the Battle of Britain Flight*
B. *Storsche spotter plane*
C. *Vulcan bomber*
D. *Lightning fighter*

40

Up went the ladders, aloft went the men, and soon the pilot was roped to a stretcher and being lowered down with rescue lines. Unknown to all, however, a six inch bolt protruded from the curved wall of the building. This pierced the fabric of the stretcher, causing the pilot to pivot on an important part of his anatomy and impress the crew with the authentic nature of his yells. He was freed before suffering any serious damage to his marriage prospects but the following year the flying fraternity showed a marked reluctance to assist the CAA Inspector, and a dummy had to be used instead.

The CAA inspection was always slightly harrowing but it was as nothing compared to the set-piece displays which the crews were frequently asked to provide for the various galas held in the villages around Hull. These displays consisted of several firefighting drills carried out in sequence, to whistle blasts, and any crewman would admit to preferring a real 'shout' any time. In a live situation you could cover your mistakes, providing you survived them. Out in the arena you never had a chance. The only answer was gruelling practice and rehearsals, and this combination worked adequately... until one day when the unexpected occurred.

The crew were in the centre of a village green arena, poised to begin the opening drill. A whistle shrilled and half the crew went into action. The other half stood fast, having recognised the source of the whistle as a youngsters' five-a-side football match elsewhere on the green. The authentic whistle came a moment later but despite their best efforts the followers remained out of synchronisation with the leaders. Gradually the display degenerated as the men ad-libbed to maintain continuity and the five-a-side whistle continued to multiply the confusion. To those sweating and cursing their way through this fiasco it seemed that the display must resemble nothing more than a demonstration of pure lunacy, but in fact the prayed-for conclusion brought enthusiastic applause. It seemed that nobody who didn't know what should have happened had any idea that it hadn't happened. It had all been done quickly and smartly, and that was sufficient to convince the audience that it had been done properly. Having experienced the worst and survived it the crew gave up worrying so much about set-piece displays, consequently the ensuing ones went like clockwork.

Some time later a local farmer had reason to be grateful that the crew worked better on real jobs. While circling the airfield, prior to landing, one of the Aero Club's pilots spotted a barn on fire below. The pilot called Air Traffic Control, which put in a 999 call, and then alerted the fire crew. The water tender was dispatched and headed towards the incident by homing in on the aircraft now circling distantly over the barn - a feat made more difficult by the fact that every road seemed to lead off in the wrong direction and the vehicle was not designed for overland travel. Eventually the crew arrived in a farmyard containing a three-bay dutch barn packed with bagged fertiliser and well-alight, and were soon joined there by the Preston retained crew. Together the two crews contained and quelled the blaze, with the retained men delivering a good-natured barracking about posh volunteers who employed aerial fire-spotting systems.

Swift response has always been a major factor in firefighting operations, for a minor outbreak can develop into a major conflagration with awesome speed. In aircraft accident work the problem is compounded by the presence of high octane fuel, a mechanical power source, electrical systems and people - all packed into an enclosed space. As someone once observed; "No building with such characteristics would get past the regulations - and then to add the final touch the damn things go up in the air !"

To ensure fast response CAP 168 sets out strict standards for vehicle performance, and a ruling that the

Above: Arriving from the past a little early... A B-17 Flying Fortress makes a low pass during an air display, to the consternation of the parachute display team caught out on the runway.

Left: *The redoubtable 'Stringbag'... A restored Fairey Swordfish prepares to taxi out for its display performance. The crowds seemed to find aircraft such as these more fascinating than their modern counterparts. Perhaps it was the astonishing realisation that men actually went to war in such fragile machines.*

crew should be capable of reaching the furthest point of the perimeter within three minutes of turn-out. To keep the crew on their toes Air Traffic Control would periodically raise a mock 'shout', choosing the nature of the emergency from the three-stage system established by Peter Metheringham.

1 AIRCRAFT LOCAL STANDBY
(An accident may occur, but probably won't).

2 AIRCRAFT FULL EMERGENCY
(An accident may not occur, but probably will).

3 AIRCRAFT ACCIDENT (Too late...).

Aircraft Local Standby's were a regular feature of life at Paull Airfield, and were usually raised unobtrusively to avoid creating general alarm. The sight of an ATC member strolling towards the crew's engine house looking deliberately unconcerned was invariably enough to lower paint brushes and polish cloths and raise resigned murmurs of "Here we go again, folks...."

The sounding of the siren, however, indicated a far greater degree of urgency and produced the kind of response that leaves coffee mugs standing in mid-air. Having now gained some ten years experience the crew could achieve a response time well within the statutory three minutes, but it fell to a particularly enthusiastic - and burly - driver, accompanied by a diminutive leading fireman, to set a new record for arrival at Air Traffic Control.

It was a peaceful Sunday afternoon and the two men were in the clubhouse waiting for the rest of the crew to come on duty. Overhead some confusion occurred, and two aircraft tried to land on the same runway simultaneously-whereupon the Chief Flying Instructor took a precautionary poke at the siren button.

What happened next is best described in the parody written later. A good tale loses nothing in the telling, they say, but even allowing for exaggeration it was quite a turnout.

THE BALLAD OF TEN-SECOND BRIAN

You could hear his big boots pound as they raced across the ground,
And the screaming of the siren as it echoed round and round,
As he galloped from the clubhouse door, his helmet in his hand,
His name was Brian and he drove the fastest Bedford in the land.

Now Brian had a mate with him, an LF swift and fleet,
He weighed six stone-seven, soaking wet, and his boots were on wrong feet.
As one they leapt into the cab and skidded on the floor,
And Brian damn-near pushed the LF out the other door.
Then the engine howled, the beacons flashed and loud the bell it pealed,
And off went Brian who drove the fastest Bedford on the field.

The Bedford swung out from its bay in a blaze of chrome and brass.
Wiped two cars off the car park and roared off across the grass,
It hurtled past the clubhouse and it bounced onto the track,
And beneath the eye of the CFI it swiped the wireless shack.
But Brian kept his foot hard down, a smile upon his face,
His name was Brian and he drove the fastest Bedford in the place.

Away beside the runway wide they shuddered to a stop,
Two planes touched down without a sound, intact from tail to prop,
And remarking that the dents they'd made could easy be repainted,
Our Brian found, to his surprise, that the LF had fainted.
But his idiot grin as he drove back in was like a flag unfurled,
His name was Brian and he drove the fastest Bedford in the world!

Speed is not everything, of course. Sometimes a more cautious approach is required - as became apparent when a private parachuting team moved onto the airfield. Over several weekends the jumpers were rescued from various parts of the countryside but it was the one who found the perimeter ditch who created the biggest problem. During his descent he had begun to swing, and by the time he neared the ground the swing had developed into pendulum-like arcs. The last of these was so extensive that it actually swung him above his own canopy - at which point the canopy went slack and hit the ground, followed seconds later by the jumper. Arrival point was the dreaded ditch, and the impact broke the jumper's pelvis and jammed him into the narrow bottom of the ditch like a cork in a bottle.

As the crew turned out to extricate him they were joined by a doctor who had been watching the distant drama from the clubhouse. As the vehicle arrived on site he jumped from it and dashed towards the casualty - only to run straight into a barbed wire fence, the barbs of which caught him across the forehead...

Both he and the jumper were duly handed over on the arrival of an ambulance.

Another jumper, a young lady, lost control of her chute in mid descent when she was caught by a sharp cross-wind. Her route took her directly across the front of the engine house, at about a hundred feet and some 30 knots. As she sailed over the heads of the gaping crew they were joined by the instructor, who bellowed instructions into the sky, but in vain. With a despairing cry of "WHAAT?" the girl vanished into a nearby copse, slammed squarely into a tree and knocked herself cold. She was rapidly retrieved from amidst the boughs and branches and recovered consciousness with just a headache and a sprained thumb to show for her adventure.

The Pitts Special regularly thrilled the crowds at Hull Air Show with its remarkable aerobatic displays.

Left: The Grumman Tiger which pancaked after its undercarriage was torn off by a runway marker seconds before touchdown. The Land Rover RIV can be seen in attendance, just beyond the nose of the aircraft. The occupants emerged from the wreck shaken but otherwise unhurt, and the 1979 Hull Air Show continued without further mishap.

The 1979 Hull Air Show was the most ambitious so far, featuring the Red Arrows, The Barnstormers and Rothmans Aerobatic Team. The displays were timed to commence at 14.00, which should have allowed the fire crew ample time to parade for inspection, briefing and the detailing of vehicle crews. Thus when the siren began its rising scream at 11.15, halfway through the inspection, the sound produced a moment of astonished paralysis before the men broke ranks and leapt aboard their vehicles. The explanation lay, flat and battered, on the runway perimeter. A single engined Grumman Tiger, delivering an air display controller from Humberside Airport, had struck one of the raised runway markers seconds before touch-down, ripping away the undercarriage and causing the aircraft to pancake ignominiously onto the runway. The pilot and passengers were recovered, shaken but unhurt, but it was necessary to leave the aircraft unmoved pending the arrival of a Civil Aviation Inspector. So there the wreckage stayed, serving as a sombre reminder for the pilots whose aerobatic exploits unfolded across the sky during the afternoon.

The Air Show itself went flawlessly, without even the need for parachutist rescue. As every motorist knows, the sight of a little wreckage concentrates the mind admirably.

A few weeks after the air display the crew were asked to provide routine cover for a Country & Western Night to be held in the airfield's main hangar. It should have been a straightforward task - a 'milk run' as they were known - but instead the event provided its own little excitement. On the night several hundred revellers packed into the hangar, which had been decorated and furnished with straw-bale seating, and which contained a flat-truck to serve as a platform for the performers. Unfortunately the generator required to power the performers' equipment had failed to arrive by early evening, so instead the hangar's normal supply was utilised - and around 10 p.m. the crew were requested to respond to the hangar's junction box, which was rapidly overheating. Concerned at the possibility of panic if the power supply failed, the officer in charge directed the crews to deploy their vehicles swiftly but unobtrusively around the open front of the hangar, then approached the scene of the overheating - but didn't make it. With a resounding bang and a blinding flash the junction box succumbed, the music died and the packed hangar was plunged into blackness. Hardly had the first female scream risen, however, when the line-up of headlights and searchlights blazed on, bathing the interior in eerie white light and de-fusing the potential panic.

With their power gone the performers transferred to acoustic guitars and the night continued to a successful conclusion. Only next day was it discovered that effects of the exploding junction box had not been confined to the hangar. Half of a neighbouring village had been blacked out as well...

During the following summer Paull Airfield was chosen to host the Amy Johnson Air Pageant, held in honour of Hull's most intrepid daughter. The event drew large crowds and was unmarred by anything other than the exhaustion of the fire crew, which carried out 48 hours of continuous standby and security duties to ensure that no harm befell the visiting aircraft, some of which dated back to the days of Amy's epic solo flight to Australia.

That summer, too, a party of enthusiasts from The Fire Brigade Society visited the airfield, and the Society's magazine 'Fire Cover' subsequently reported *'The Paul Airfield fire crew are to be admired for their enthusiasm and the way in which their appliances have been brought to their present immaculate condition.'*

It helped to make up for the Lord Mayor's Parade.

But if the darkest hour comes just before dawn, the brightest comes just before darkness descends - and descend it promptly did. Towards the end of the year it was announced that the Hull Aero Club had been unable to secure a renewal of their lease and consequently the airfield would close during the following spring

A second blow followed, with the death of the Association's most senior member, George E. Watkinson. 'Ernie', as he was affectionately known, had been the senior ranking officer of Hull's Auxiliary Fire Service at the time of the disbandment, having worked his way up through the ranks since 1948 - in the course of which ascent he had led the competition team which won the Hebden-Royd Trophy. A mild, gentlemanly man, he had served as the Association's first secretary, framing the constitution upon which its activities were based. Later he became the Association's first president, and although in later years ill-health had forced him to abandon operational participation he was always available to offer wise and moderate council.

Now, faced with the extinction of its home base, the Paull Airfield Auxiliary Fire Section could hardly have needed Ernie's guidance more. They were facing a replay of 1968 but with added complications. Then they had been left only with their uniforms. Now they were vehicled and equipped - very much a case of being 'all dressed up and nowhere to go'.

Gradually the airfield began to die. The last of Bristow's helicopters lifted-off and flew away, winter closed icily over the runways and as the weeks passed the position began to look increasingly hopeless.

Then the legacy of Flixborough came to the rescue. Shortly after the disaster Humberside County Council had established a department responsible for producing plans and compiling information which would be required in the event of any similar disaster. Known simply as the Emergency Planning Service, this department was, by 1980, under the control of Eric Alley; an internationally recognised authority on civil defence work and a staunch believer in the value of volunteers. By sheer coincidence the crew had arranged to visit the headquarters of the Emergency Planning Service to find out how civil defence matters had developed since their departure from the field in 1968. Meeting Eric Alley during this visit they enquired whether he might have a use for a homeless fire crew and found him enthusiastic about the possibilities There followed a brief burst of correspondence and within a

The final vehicle line-up at the closure of Paull Airfield in 1980. The combination of these four vehicles gave Paull Airfield a standard of emergency cover far in excess of the requirements for its catagory.

Left: Land Rover purchased by Hull Aero Club as a replacement for the ageing Austin Gypsy, and transformed by the Association into a Rapid Intervention Vehicle equipped for pilot rescue.

Right: Bedford Foam Tender formerly owned by British Aerospace and purchased by Hull Aero Club.

Right: The Association's Bedford water tender.

Left: The Austin control unit.

matter of days the County Council had granted permission for the crew to transfer its resources to the EPS Headquarters - a former civil defence complex in the village of Wawne, just outside the city - there to re-establish as a new volunteer emergency team to assist the EPS and the community as and when requested.

It appeared to be a dream solution to the nightmare problem of finding a home.

Despite the promise of the new situation it was a wrench, leaving the airfield which had been home for over ten years. It was a wrench to say farewell to the Blackburn Beverley Freighter, which had become like a huge old friend. The crew might well have felt better had they known that it would eventually be carefully dismantled and then lovingly rebuilt as an exhibit in the Museum of Army Transport, at Beverley. On a more practical level it was a wrench to lose the foam tender and the Land Rover. These, being the property of Hull Aero Club, were sold off to other airfields.

The water tender and the control unit, together with a recently acquired trailer pump, were loaded with the accumulated equipment and materials of years, and at 15.30 hours on the afternoon of Sunday, 22nd March 1981 the crew drove from Paull Airfield for the last time, en-route for the headquarters of the Emergency Planning Service.

At 24.00 hours on March 31st 1981 Paull Airfield Auxiliary Fire Section ceased to exist. In total, 24 men and women had kept the unit operational since its formation, all with a minimum of outside assistance.

On the 1st April 1981 the Humberside Auxiliary Emergency Service came into being

It was precisely 13 years to the day since the disbandment of the Auxiliary Fire Service.

The last duty crew parades before the main hangar for a farewell photograph after the final stand-by at Paull Airfield.

49

HUMBERSIDE AUXILIARY EMERGENCY SERVICE - WAWNE

The complex which housed the Emergency Planning Service - soon to become known simply as 'the Centre'-was a former Civil Defence Corps command post located in the village of Wawne. For many years rumour had designated the place as a bolt-hole for bureaucrats wishing to escape the nuclear holocaust. In fact it was simply being utilised due to a shortage of office space at County Hall, Beverley, and in fact, as the arriving HAES crew discovered, it had approximately the same protective qualities as a fairly sturdy garden shed. Following the 1968 disbandment the structure had been left derelict for several years, after which partial renovation had made it suitable for administrative use. The labrynth of offices did at least extend to basement level, but there the bolt-hole qualities ceased. There was no separate water supply, no air filtration or purification system and the telephone system operated through the normal city exchange. There was even a duct in the ceiling of the crew's basement room which led directly into the open air - it became standard practice to feed a cable through it to charge the batteries of the vehicles standing outside in the compound. As someone remarked: "Only a nut would choose this place as a bolt-hole!"

Before the basement room - Room 20 - could be occupied it was necessary to empty it, and the contents proved evocative. Here were boxes crammed with documents and photographs from the pre-disbandment days, and cartons crammed with silver cups and trophies won in various competitions by the Hull Civil Defence Corps.

A nissen hut in the compound was also allocated to the crew, and the 'finds' continued - in this case a mass of field catering equipment once intended for the emergency feeding of refugees and now rusted and battered beyond repair.

Gradually Room 20 and the nissen hut were cleared. The former was redecorated and transformed into a crew room, the latter became a workshop and equipment store. A training schedule was implemented and the crew began to shake down in their new surroundings and catch up on the current civil defence situation. It was not an inspiring exercise.

Since the disbandment of 1968 civil defence had been left to individual local authorities, some of whom accepted the need for it, some of whom definitely did not. Accordingly there had developed a disparate collection of local systems and non-systems which in total were inferior to the civilian protection systems operated by all other European nations and most of the Third World countries.

A new identity demands a new image, and to avoid any confusion with the regular fire service the Association decreed that the vehicles of the Humberside Auxiliary Emergency Service should have a lime green livery. First to receive the treatment was the water tender, and the effect was undeniably eye-catching.

In a bid to rationalise the shambles the incoming Conservative government had appointed Sir Leslie Mavor as 'Co-ordinator of Voluntary Effort in Civil Defence', his role being to establish a unified framework within which volunteer units could operate to assist their communities. So far his efforts had been hampered by problems ranging from the Home Office's inability to define training standards for volunteers, to the belief by many local authorities that supporting volunteer emergency workers was somehow incompatible with their status as Nuclear Free Zones.

Against this background HAES took its place as the fifth element in the County's volunteer emergency system; joining the Red Cross, the St John Ambulance Brigade, the WRVS and RAYNET. It was noted by some members that there had once been a far simpler system for responding to emergencies. An authentic sign on one of the office walls attested to the fact:

With the days of aircraft accidents behind them the crews now had to learn the skills required for their 'general emergency' role, and began participating in joint exercises with other volunteer organisations such as the Red Cross, St John Ambulance and Territorial Army. The exercise shown here centred around a simulated industrial explosion which produced the need to rescue casualties from high heights and tight corners.

Following the departure of the old water tender in 1983 a 'new' one was purchased from the North Yorkshire Fire Authority. By its nature a fire appliance travels a relatively short distance during its lifetime, and so can offer many years good service even when purchased second-hand. Coming complete with Ajax extension ladder and Light Portable Pump, the new acquisition provided a good operational capability.

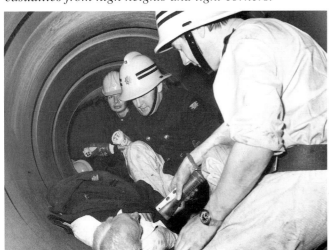

MOBILISATION & MOVEMENT ORDER 1935 by The EMPEROR HAILE SELASSIE

1 When this order is received all men and boys able to carry a spear will go to Addis Ababa.

2 Every married man will bring his wife to cook and wash for him.

3 Every unmarried man will bring an unmarried woman to cook and wash for him.

4 Women with babies, the blind and those too aged or infirm to carry a spear are excluded.

5 Anyone found at home after receiving this order will be killed.

It soon became clear that the situation at Wawne would not yield to such a simple approach.

It had been hoped to garage the vehicles in the Centre's huge aircraft hangar-like garage but it was now discovered this building had been taken over by the County Supplies Department for the storage of school exercise books. Eric Alley began negotiations but in the meantime it was necessary to remove all equipment from the vehicles and store it in the nissen hut for security.

This proved to be a mistake. One evening, late in the year, the nissen hut was broken into and a large quantity of equipment stolen. Two breathing apparatus sets, aircraft axes, first aid kits, complete vehicle tool kits... these and many other hard-won items vanished. The remaining equipment was transferred into Room 20 for safety, and despite the congestion the crew continued to soldier on - in one case literally.

This was 'Joint-Stock', a combined exercise held in conjunction with the St. John Ambulance Brigade and the Territorial Army amidst the ruins of Paull Fort. Built during the First World War to house the shore batteries charged with keeping the Humber free of Teutonic warships the fort proved the ideal setting for a simulated terrorist attack on a major barracks - with a toxic chemical spill thrown in for good measure. Throughout the afternoon the crew tackled fire and spillage and lowered stretchered casualties down from the towering battlements while around them platoons of sweating soldiers raced backwards and forwards, raked the area with machine gun fire and launched thunderflash and tear gas attacks. Inevitably the element of comedy crept into the proceedings, via a wounded soldier who had to be lowered from the battlements down a circular shaft - a shaft so narrow that it was necessary to lash the casualty to a stretcher and lower him down feet-first. All went well until the half-way point, when the stretcher began to rotate on its ropes; slowly at first, then with ever-increasing speed. Trussed up and trapped between heaven and earth the luckless soldier could only watch as the iron rungs inside the shaft whipped past his nose at ever increasing speed, while above and below him cursing firemen struggled to control his flat spin. Eventually the crew succeeded in getting him safely down, whereupon he rejoined the war with obvious relief.

As if to balance the account the following month brought a further exercise which took a greater toll on rescuers than casualties. The setting was the Hull Fish Meal plant on Alexandra Dock, where members of the Casualty Union were draped and horrifically made-up as the burned victims of an industrial explosion. The HAES crew had encountered the Casualty Union and their convincingly gruesome injuries in the past, and it was generally accepted that if they failed to make a rescuer throw up they felt they had failed. On this occasion they succeeded better than usual. Two of the more enterprising members had lodged themselves high on a catwalk directly above an operating industrial boiler, forcing the rescuing crew to operate in conditions that could not have been bettered in a sauna. Weighed down with equipment, and steaming in their heavy uniforms, the crew valiantly scaled the heights and lowered the realistically-shrieking casualties down... after which two of them passed out from heat exhaustion!

Meanwhile the problem of the garage proved intractable and by the end of 1982 the control unit had succumbed to the elements and had to be scrapped. It was a depressing blow which reflected, in microcosm, a nationwide problem. During that year the government had attempted to carry out a national civilian protection exercise designated 'Hard Rock', but had been forced to abandon the project as too many local authorities were unable to show any operational capability, even in the evacuation of civilians from danger areas.

A replacement for the control unit was sought, and the Hull-based pharmaceutical group Reckitt a Colman came to the rescue. The company possessed a small, custom-built fire appliance that was no longer required, and this was generously allocated to the crew on a 'permanent loan' basis. It was rapidly re-equipped, sprayed in the distinctive lime green livery which the Association had now adopted to prevent confusion with the professional fire brigade, and made operational as an emergency tender. And just in time.

On the night of 1st/2nd February 1983 high winds and storm tides brought flooding to many parts of the East Coast. Out in the North Sea the MV *Norland* was struggling to reach Hull and a civic reception after its adventures in the Falklands conflict, while on the nearby coast, at Hornsea, the emergency tender's crew was wading thigh-deep in freezing water as they struggled to assist those whose homes had been engulfed. It was a night of bitter cold, arduous effort and memorable lines

A builder's merchant, roused at midnight to open his yard to provide sand for the sandbags, eyed the unfamiliar HAES uniforms and remarked: 'I can see all sorts of pips and bars and things - but who's got the authority to sign a bill for this bloody lot!'

A housewife, perched high on her staircase watched the crew slosh into her home through two feet of muddy water and directed: 'Wipe your feet, lads, there's a lovely carpet under there'

Left: Custom-built as an 'in-house' fire appliance for Reckitt and Colman Ltd, this unique vehicle was presented to the Association on permanent loan in 1982, and brought into service as an emergency tender. The outward impression of a standard commercial van is deceptive; the rear double doors open onto a firefighting pump, and a centrally-mounted interior hosereel can be fed out through a small porthole on either side. Fitted with a wide range of equipment including a portable generator and floodlights, the vehicle first saw service during floods at Hornsea.

"We saw it coming and ran to the police station," said one old lady, with forlorn and unconscious humour, "but it shuts at five-o'-clock".

In one bungalow the crew encountered an elderly couple who, in the best Blitz tradition, steadfastly refused to move, despite the fact that encroaching water had turned their electrical supply into a crackling blue firework display. All that could be done was to sandbag their doors and call in the Electricity Board to isolate the place - then on to a lady whose horses were becoming increasingly frantic in their steadily-sinking stable...

With communications provided by Raynet, the crew worked until the small hours, finally returning wet and weary to the Centre.

It had been a muddy christening for the new vehicle.

The christening was followed by a funeral. The garage problem could not be resolved, and two winters in the open proved too much for the water tender; ice cracked both the cylinder head and the casing of the firefighting pump. Ironically, within a few days of the damage being discovered the vehicle was limped into the garage, there to expire. The threat of a water-workers dispute had enabled Eric Alley to gain permission for the vehicle to be garaged, so its 400-gallon tank could be used as a static water supply. So the defunct vehicle was now moved into the garage among the exercise books while the operational one had to remain outside...

Within weeks a replacement water tender had been obtained from the North Yorkshire Fire Authority. The purchase almost wiped out the Association's funds but was vital if the operational section was to continue operating. And despite disappointments and setbacks the determination to continue was still there, as the Secretary's Annual Report, presented in May 1983, indicates:

"The year which closes tonight is the fifteenth since the formation of our Association, and the second year of our efforts to establish a volunteer emergency unit on Humberside. To some extent it has been a disappointing year. I note, however, that both the current issue of the Municipal Yearbook and the latest report from the National Co-ordinator for Voluntary Effort in Civil Defence reflect disappointing results in this field, which seems to indicate that our slow progress is not so much the result of our own deficiencies but the symptom of a national problem."

"Despite this the last twelve months has seen an increase in the momentum of our activities. Two combined exercises were undertaken with the St John Ambulance Brigade, we played a useful role in the Territorial Army Exercise 'Joint-Stock'83' and were able to participate in joint training and film sessions with the Red Cross. Standby and display duties were carried out for a number of organisations during the year, and personnel were provided during the Emergency Planning Department's oil pollution demonstration on the coast. Additionally we were called upon to undertake flood relief work during February - an operation which gained the Association an official commendation from the county's Public Protection Committee."

"Like the tip of an iceberg such activities are merely the visible aspect of a far greater amount of concealed support and administrative effort. The negotiations for, and subsequent renovation and re-equipping of, the emergency tender kindly supplied by Reckitt & Colman took up up much time and effort and the members involved are to be commended - as are those currently undertaking renovation of the trailer pump. The programme of equipment maintenance has continued steadily, and acquisitions during the year have included a comprehensive vehicle tool kit, new display boards, an ample supply of rescue line, and vehicle batteries kindly donated by the Emergency Planning Service. And during this final month we have, of course, succeeded in securing an additional vehicle. Once again our thanks go to all who have put time and effort into preparing this new vehicle for its operational function."

"Such material gains have in turn been supported by a variety of administrative achievements, ranging from the establishment of a systemised training schedule to the introduction of a much-improved personal accident insurance scheme. As always, of course, there were those administrative efforts which went unrewarded, but were nevertheless worth the endeavour. Despite two lengthy attempts the committee failed to secure grant support from the government, and a direct approach to the Prime Minister for the allocation of a Bedford 'Green Goddess' self-propelled pump was referred to the Home Office and thus ultimately rejected."

"On the social side we have been quite successful. Our own functions were well-attended and enjoyed. As a result of our attendance at a joint St John Ambulance Territorial Army social earlier this year we were able to submit a good donation to the Retained Firefighters Union appeal for those Australian fire fighters killed during the recent bush fire disaster. Several members also attended the annual reunion of the Yorkshire Auxiliary Fire Service Association."

"Continuing operational problems have made it necessary to adopt a low profile in terms of public relations this year, although our activities were featured in the house magazine of Reckitt & Colman, in the Scarborough Evening News and twice in the Hull Daily Mail. Arrangements are currently in hand for a feature to appear in 'Fire Cover', the journal of the Fire Brigade Society."

"Unquestionably the most regrettable aspect of the past year has been the loss of those two appliances which accompanied us from Paull Airfield. The arrival of the new first line vehicle should go some way to alleviate the effects of this dual loss, but it goes without saying that a repetition of this event must be avoided, and that a swift and permanent solution to the garaging problem must be a No. 1 priority for the incoming committee."

"In concluding this report I would draw members' attention to one major point. When this Association was first formed we possessed only our uniforms and a determination to serve the community. We now have an impressive array of resources with which to pursue that aim. We have gained them through our own sacrifices and efforts, and over the years have overcome major obstacles through dedication, expertise and plain hard work. Obviously it is confusing to find that application of these qualities no longer automatically brings success, but in the transition from a self-contained unit - as we were at Paull Airfield - to being a tiny part of a local authority system, we were perhaps bound to encounter obstacles that held out against our rather simple and straight forward approach. I have every confidence that we shall still overcome them."

Confidence remained high throughout 1983, for although such problems as garage accommodation remained unsolved the crew had little time to brood upon them, being involved in a large number of exercises and training schemes, including Community Adviser's Courses - aimed basically at those civilians now being recruited to assist their communities in times of emergency-practical firemanship and breathing apparatus courses, and - for Chief Officer Peter Metheringham - a week's course at the Home Defence

College at Easingwold, which provided significant. information on proposed new plans to re-establish some form of national civil defence system.

Having now settled into its new home the service began to receive an increasing number of requests for displays and standby duties at various local functions. Usually such events were simply an opportunity to let youngsters sit in the cab of a fire appliance, or spray a little water around with stirrup pumps, but one that year - the annual Princess Royal Hospital Gala - produced its own set of problems and went down as the wettest duty ever done that wasn't actually a flood job.

The rain commenced on the night before the gala, while the crew were providing overnight security and fire cover for the conglomeration of stalls and marquees. During the following morning the torrent increased and by lunchtime several stalls had collapsed under the weight of water. Attempts by stall holders to retrieve their wares led to several vehicles becoming bogged down, while others simply stalled as water seeped into their engines - the combination keeping the crews busy with jack plates, ropes and jump leads. Early afternoon brought a lull in the sheeting rain, tempting massed ranks of majorettes out for a march past. Their courage was undeniable but their optimism misplaced. No sooner were the brightly-costumed battalions assembled than the heavens opened, delivering a downpour that dwarfed anything which had gone before. Under this onslaught. the massed ranks broke in confusion and for the next twenty minutes the cursing, dripping crewmen were retrieving sodden baton-twirlers and saturated kazzoo players from the mud and carrying them to shelter.

The end of that year came in fittingly soggy manner. At 4 p.m. on Friday December 9th HAES members were called out to attend a flooding incident... at the Emergency Planning Service headquarters, Wawne.

After 48 hours of rain, water was draining from surrounding fields and rising in the offices on the lower level. Utilising the water tender's main and lightweight pumps the crew succeeded in emptying the building's main overflow sump, thus preventing further flooding. The sump continued to refill, however, and had to be pumped out several more times. Shortly after midnight the situation was stabilised and the crew stood down - only to be turned out again an hour later.

This time the incident centred around Lapwing Close, on the Bransholme Estate, where a combination of the rain and a pumping station failure had filled streets and homes with icy, muddy-brown torrents. Their vehicles laden with sandbags, the crew rendezvoused with a council lorry loaded with sand and began securing the houses in the area while a shuttle of ambulances evacuated old people. Some time later two regular fire brigade appliances arrived and a combined operation developed, as did a quantity of good natured barracking centring mainly on the presence of an operational firewoman in the HAES ranks - a rare novelty for the regular brigade. One regular brigade officer was taken so much by surprise that on arrival he swept his torch beam across the crew shovelling sand from the lorry and announced in awed tones; "Jesus - it's Snow White and the Seven Dwarfs..."

By the early hours of the morning the situation was under control, the water level began to fall and at 7 a.m. the crews were able to stand down and return to Emergency Planning Service headquarters - there to be served a breakfast of bacon and eggs cooked by the hand of the Senior Emergency Planning Officer himself, Eric Alley.

The incident brought a further letter of thanks and commendation from the County's Public Protection Committee, which praised the 'enthusiasm, discipline and skill shown by all the volunteers'. It was a gesture that was appreciated but, as someone pointed out, a key to the garage would have been preferred.

During the course of 1983 the Government had introduced new Civil Defence legislation, specifically the Civil Defence (Local Authority Functions) Act. Among other things this required that local authorities should encourage volunteers in the emergency field, and should establish volunteer rescue teams capable of mobilisation within seven days if required. Unfortunately no material now existed for the training of such rescue teams and accordingly, early in 1984, HAES were approached by the Emergency Planning Service to make a video film which could be used to train other volunteers.

The Association agreed and, under the direction of a member of the EPS staff, the members embarked on a crash training course in rescue techniques. Throughout the summer they practiced knots and linework endlessly, learned to secure collapsing structures, retrieved casualties from rooftops and rubble and stretchered them endlessly across rough terrain, down staircases and through the solid blackness of the centre's basement.

The completion of the course was marked by Exercise Alpha, undertaken before representatives of the County Council and members of the Mines Rescue Service. Based on an authentic incident involving a goods train explosion in a built-up area the exercise required the location, treatment and rescue of four individuals trapped underground and under debris somewhere in the Centre's maze of basement corridors. This was successfully achieved but in the heat of an August night, and with the crews burdened with full rescue kit, the exercise was like a strenuous version of a sauna. Subsequently the crew retired to The Waggoners hostelry in Wawne, to pick the brains of the Mines Rescue team and drink pints that never touched the sides.

With the training complete, it was now necessary to locate a suitable setting for the filming. As on previous occasions, politics provided the stumbling block. An application was made to the Hull City Council Housing Committee for the use of a suitably derelict building - and was promptly rejected because of one committee member's contention that 'only war and bombs damaged houses, and people shouldn't prepare for such events.' Within 24 hours the fatuousness of that remark was brought home as a Nottinghamshire village was wrecked by a tornado, and 90 minutes of severe rainfall brought havoc to Hull, but fatuous or not, the decision remained. Eventually a row of derelict houses was discovered in Hedon, and these were preserved for posterity by the camera just before the bulldozers moved in.

A Tuesday evening exercise at Weel Bridge, Beverley Beck, bringing the major pump and Light Portable Pump into action on opposite banks. Such exercises provided new recruits with useful training in both pump operating and branch-holding.

The cameraman was almost not preserved for posterity. The proposed content of the film required that some casualties be rescued from upper floors - a hazardous undertaking since most of the floors had collapsed into the rooms below. The rescuers could at least watch their footing as they worked their way along the beams, but the cameraman was forced to keep his eyes to the viewfinder. Accordingly a crewman was detailed to hang on to the cameraman's belt at all times, and was fortunately doing exactly that when the man stepped into thin air... He was dragged up through the smashed floor with all but his dignity intact, the moment of his departure caught on film as a whirl of plunging camera and a view of the roof overhead spinning and receding.

It was a bitterly cold day and in view of this Chief Officer Peter Metheringham for once relaxed his long-established ruling that the HAES uniform should never be seen on licensed premises. Approaching the landlord of a nearby pub he requested that his crews be allowed inside to eat their sandwiches. Permission was granted but the landlord must have wondered what he had let himself in for when through the door trooped a stream of firefighters, rescue workers, film technicians and casualties - the latter cheerfully sporting plastic injuries gory enough to put anyone off their pub lunch.

By the end of the afternoon the crews were exhausted and grimy but the film was in the can. It seemed little to show for so many months of rigorous training but the skills gained during that period were valuable in themselves, and the crew could only hope that the result of their efforts would prove to be of use to others like themselves.

Despite the demands of the rescue training course the Association managed to satisfy requests for attendance at several local galas and shows during that summer, and was able to assist the organisers of the Cottingham Show by pumping thousands of gallons of water from the flooded showground, thereby ensuring, in the best showbusiness tradition, that the Show could go on. Another standby duty undertaken that summer was for the Grand Annual Summer Charity Feast of the Wilberforce Round Table and Haltemprice Lions Club. The event was held at Raywell Park on Friday 21st June, and continued until the small hours of the morning. As luck would have it the crew were scheduled to take part in a joint exercise with the St. John Ambulance Brigade on the Saturday, and since there was no time either to return their vehicles to the Centre or themselves to their beds, the crew slept briefly amid the hay bales in one of the marquees before setting off for the exercise site at the premises of J.H. Fenner, Marfleet.

Improvisation in action... having used up all available stretchers, a crew utilises a ladder section to recover a casualty during a joint exercise with the St. John Ambulance Brigade at the premises of the Hull Fish Meal Company on St. Andrew's Dock.

58

Inevitably the exercise turned out to be one of the most complex and gruelling ever undertaken, the scenario including a simultaneous industrial fire, toxic chemical spill and road traffic accident. Casualties were provided by Casualty Union, who gleefully produced grisly simulations of everything from heart-attacks to crush injuries. All the incidents were effectively dealt with and certainly the months of rescue training proved their worth - although it is probable that the Casualty Union contingent would have been slightly less gleeful had they realised that the crew lowering from rooftops and jacking them out from under wreckage were doing so in a grey haze of exhaustion and were operating mostly on automatic.

The summer closed with a happy event and the resurrection of a once popular Fire Brigade tradition that is nowadays rarely seen. On a sunny Saturday in August a Leading Fireman and his new bride emerged from Holderness Road Methodist Church to find a guard-of-honour drawn up, in full uniform, and the water tender - gleaming and resplendent with white satin-draped cab waiting to carry them to the reception at the Good Fellowship Inn. Organised as meticulously as any exercise the operation went without a hitch, adding a unique element to the Association's scrapbook and the couple's wedding album.

The year that followed was one of increasing frustration terminating in tragedy. The Association lost a staunch supporter with the departure of Eric Alley to the Civil Defence Department of the Home Office, and despite the best efforts of the Emergency Planning Service it proved impossible to secure permission for the Association's appliances to be housed in the Centre's garage.

Maintaining their appearance and roadworthiness now became a full time job. At the same time a survey of the Centre itself concluded that major renovation was required in order to bring the complex up to the standard required for an emergency planning headquarters - and as the renovation commenced the crew were forced to evacuate Room 20 and move into the nissen hut workshop, which was equipped with neither power nor sanitation.

Nevertheless the Association struggled on, continuing to provide displays and undertake standby duties for various organisations throughout Hull. Then, on July 11th 1986 the Association was stunned by the sudden death of Peter Metheringhem. Peter, an electronic engineer by profession, had served as the Association's senior operational officer since 1968, commanding the operational section in all of its guises. He was well-liked and greatly respected by all who served under him, both the officers and men alike, and his loss was a great blow to the Association.

Peter Metheringham's position as officer-in-charge was now taken by Peter Blake, who had served as deputy chief for several years. The new chief took up the baton just in time to meet the gravest crisis to hit the Association in many years. With the renovation of the Centre had come a re-definition of its role, and the new role did not include housing operational units of any type.

Yet again the Association was facing eviction, and homelessness.

Efforts were made to secure alternative city or county council premises, but none were available. Thus early in 1987 the Association were only to glad to accept an invitation to garage their vehicles in a disused barn at Park Farm, on the Burton Constable Estate. It proved to be an expensive mistake. Within a month a crew arriving for Sunday training discovered that the barn had been broken into, an attempt had been made to 'hot-wire' the water tender and drive it away, and when this had failed the intruders had vandalised both vehicles finally discharging dry powder extinguishers into the cabs.

In that dark hour there came to the rescue an old friend from the past. Terry Rawson, once a regular flyer from Paull Airfield, was now creating an Air Park at Sproatley Grange. Hearing of the Association's predicament he extended an invitation for the members to join him there and establish an operational base.

It was with a collective sigh of relief that the members accepted the invitation. Early in April 1987 the two battered appliances limped from Park Farm to their new home, and before the end of the month all equipment had been transferred from Wawne.

Now it was a matter of beginning again, again.

HUMBERSIDE AUXILIARY EMERGENCY SERVICE - SPROATLEY

It might have been a case of beginning again, again, but this time there was a difference in atmosphere. Since the departure of Eric Alley the Association had felt like an administrative problem that nobody in officialdom knew how to resolve. At Sproatley Air Park the crew's presence and capabilities were appreciated, and the basic requirements for re-establishment were presented at high-speed, with no bureaucratic restrictions.

Within a week of its arrival the Association was provided with a large caravan which could be transformed into a crew room, and - most important of all - a small disused aircraft hangar which would provide shelter for the vehicles. Work on the renovation of these two buildings began immediately, as did work to repair the damage suffered by the vehicles. It would be tedious to list the work undertaken during that first year at Sproatley - as tedious as the work itself was laborious. Suffice to say that every trade and skill represented by the membership was brought into play, and twelve months later the Association could boast a smart crew room, complete with kitchen facilities, and two fully-restored appliances housed in a three-bay fire station with an integral equipment store.

During this period the effects of the Government's 1983 Civil Defence legislation at last began to be felt, and the Association was able to obtain, via the County Emergency Planning Service, a small monthly grant towards their costs. It was the first regular financial assistance to be received since the Association's formation.

The work involved in re-establishing at Sproatley largely prevented the Association from undertaking outside duties during 1987 and 1988, however it was able to contribute much in the way of uniform, equipment and photographs for the Auxiliary Fire Service section of the museum within Humberside's new Fire Brigade Headquarters at Hessle, and was also able to establish a link with the German Free Fire Service. In August 1988 six members of the Association accepted an invitation to visit Bad Oldesloe, in West Germany, for five days, taking with them letters of greeting from Hull's Lord Mayor and a City of Hull flag. In Bad Oldesloe the crew received VIP treatment, and arrangements were made for a return visit by German firefighters.

Operationally, during this period, the Association was able to provide emergency cover at several local functions and assisted the police with traffic control during the Humbrol disaster.

The creation of a three-bay station for a two appliance organisation was not simply wishful thinking. The invitation to establish at Sproatley Air Park carried with it no obligation to provide emergency cover but the Association was naturally keen to provide such a service and could do so effectively only with a Rapid-Intervention Vehicle capable of all-terrain travel. The chances of obtaining one of these seemed very slim, but then assistance came from Mr Ron Ducker, a local businessman who had been made an honorary member of the German Free Fire Service for the assistance he had rendered while working on the Continent. With the aid of an interest free loan from Mr Ducker the Association was able to obtain an ex-military long-wheelbase Land Rover, which was then transformed to give it the necessary firefighting and rescue capability.

The vehicle was complete by the spring of 1989, in time to undertake its first duty; a two-day standby for the Sproatley Air Park 'Fly-In', which attracted visiting aircraft from all over the U.K. - followed a week later by the Burton Constable Air Display. Both events passed off without incident, and what with wing-walkers and aerobatics it was all rather reminiscent of the Paull Airfield days.

It became more so during the ensuing months for although Sproatley Air Park lacked Paull's perimeter ditch it had something equally interesting - an ability to become totally fogbound in about thirty seconds. The phenomenon first occurred early one Sunday evening, bringing the crew to standby for an aircraft which had been on final approach when its destination suddenly vanished in a grey blur. The aircraft subsequently diverted to Kirmington and the crew's description of the incident was greeted with a certain derision by those members not on duty at the time - however the derision vanished the following Sunday when a fresh crew encountered the identical experience: one moment clear skies and bright sunshine, then within seconds a wall of fog driving in from the East to blanket everything. It was a hazard to be reckoned with, and one which ensured careful checking of searchlights and floodlights when each crew came on duty.

In the summer of 1989 the Association played host to some 16 members of the German Free Fire Service; a reciprocal gesture for the HAES visit to Bad Oldesloe the previous year. During their five-day visit the German party were officially welcomed by the Lord Mayors of Hull and of York, and were able to see demonstrations of British firefighting and rescue techniques at fire stations in York, Scarborough and Preston, and at Humberside Airport.

The HAES demonstration was scheduled to take place at Sproatley Air Park on the final day of the visit, and was to be followed by a farewell buffet prior to the guests' departure for the ferry terminal. With the guests due to arrive at Sproatley at 1 p.m. the HAES crews mustered four hours earlier to ensure that all preparations

for the demonstration were complete and all vehicles, equipment and uniform were smart enough to impress the invariably immaculate Germans. As noon approached the final preparations were complete... at which point Sod's Law asserted itself: before the very eyes of the waiting crews a light aircraft touched down on the runway and promptly flipped onto its back.

Off went the siren and off went the crews, arriving at the incident just as the pilot crawled from his inverted cockpit, shaken but otherwise unhurt.

It was now necessary to maintain standby until photographs of the incident had been taken, and to assist as a crane was brought up and the wreck winched back onto its wheels and towed ignominiously away. Inevitably it was a steaming hot day, and it was thus a sweating and dishevelled crew who eventually greeted the German visitors, and who had promptly to carry out the arranged demonstration for their benefit. It was a successful demonstration, commencing with a controlled explosion and incorporating everything from a foam attack on blazing oil to the rescue of a casualty from a rooftop - but to the crews it was something of an anti-climax after the real thing.

Nor was the day's excitement over. Having enjoyed the farewell buffet and exchanged gifts with the German party, the crews escorted the visitors to their ferry before returning to Sproatley to tidy up. Scarcely had they returned when a lightning bolt struck a field on the airfield perimeter, setting fire to the grass - which in turn set fire to a combine harvester operating there. The vehicles rolled for the second time that day, and the blaze was extinguished before the arrival of the regular brigade

That evening a barbecue was held at Sproatley for all who had helped to make the visit of the German party such a success, and the day proved to have one last sting in the tail. As the crews returned home through Bilton they were witness to a road accident and took control at the scene until the emergency services arrived.

All in all it had been, as someone remarked, 'One hell of a day'.

Autumn brought a 'hell of a night' to match it, for on Friday 20th October an original World War II searchlight was established in Hull's Queen Victoria Square as part of a charity nostalgia evening at the City Hall. Into the beam of that searchlight were supposed to fly a an RAF helicopter from Leconfield and a Tobago aircraft from Sproatley Air Park. By early evening the weather conditions were atrocious, with torrential rain and gale force winds, and the crew accordingly turned out to provide emergency cover for the Tobago's takeoff and - if that was achieved - its subsequent landing. In the event the conditions prevented take-off, the RAF helicopter was diverted to an emergency incident and the searchlight was left to shine alone while the crew hung around drinking tea, loth to leave in case the storm brought need for their services or the removal of their combined weight caused the crewroom to blow away...

By the spring of 1990 Sproatley Air Park had become very much a 'home from home', complete with the kind of comforts that are taken for granted in most organisations but which were a novelty to an organisation which had moved around too often in the past to get properly established. A TV, fridge and cooker in the crew room, a trophy cabinet for displaying the gifts from Germany, even simply a filing cabinet for the paperwork... these things provided a much-needed feeling of permanence. Standby duties and static displays were now being undertaken with increasing frequency and it was becoming clear that a recruitment drive was needed if the same crews were to be spared having to be on duty over several successive weekends. But hardly had that option been raised when, in May, the much-needed feeling of permanence suddenly evaporated.

It was announced that, owing to a change of property ownership, Sproatley Air Park would close by the end of June.

'Heartbreaking' has got to be too mild a description for the impact of this announcement. Three years of hard work nullified by a change of circumstances. On the other hand it was generally agreed that those three years at Sproatley had been among the most enjoyable in the Association's history. The setting had been right, the need for the Association's services was there and the commitment from the crews had been superb.

But now it was time to move on once more, and it had to be done fast. With no other options available, the Association accepted the only offer put forward, and on June 23rd 1990 its vehicles and equipment travelled in sad cavalcade to the premises of Hedon Growers in the village of Burstwick, there to be stored until the future brought some opportunity for re-establishment in an operational setting.

The first standby duty at Sproatley Air Park was for the inaugural flight of this tiny Taylor Monoplane, built during an eight-year period by brothers Gerald and Geoff Ward. The flight went without a hitch and the aircraft became a regular feature at Sproatley. Note the specially obtained registration.

Refurbished and repainted by HAES members, the caravan donated by Mr T. Rawson at Sproatley Air Park was transformed into a very serviceable crew room/control room. Also donated was a former aircraft hangar that was became a three-bay station.

Right: Foam drill training, using a 5x foam branch and an induction tube to a drum of foam compound. Experience showed that a length of hose kept permanently 'flaked' at the back of the vehicle could be utilised much more rapidly than a normal 'rolled' length, and using this system it proved possible to get foam onto an incident within 30 seconds of arrival.

Left: Practicing the removal of an unconscious casualty from the roof of the crewroom. The role of casualty usually fell to one of the Association's ladies, who rose - or descended - to the occasion with great fortitude. Being lowered off a roof while roped helplessly to a stretcher is an exercise which demands a certain faith on the part of the victim.

Left: A vehicle capable of all-terrain travel is essential for airfield work, and accordingly in 1989 the Association acquired a standard long-wheelbase Land Rover and transformed it into a Rapid Intervention Vehicle. As always such work was carried out by the Association itself. Materials were purchased from the funds accumulated from members' weekly subscriptions, and the work was undertaken by those individuals with the necessary expertise.

Right: A Sunday afternoon duty crew, at readiness. On the left is Peter Blake who took over as over as officer in charge following the death of Peter Metheringham.

Above: *Visiting firemen... Members of the Bad Oldesloe Brigade of the German Free Fire Service during their visit to Sproatley Air Park during the summer of 1989.*

Below: *Crews lined up for inspection during the visit of firemen from the German Free Fire Service, Bad Oldesloe. The visitors were impressed by the crew's display performance but somewhat bemused by the organisation's struggle-filled history. "Only you British would be crazy enough to keep going under these conditions." one remarked. "In Germany it could not be." The crew took it as a compliment.*

Above: H.A.E.S. Chief Officer P.S. Blake presents the Service's plaque to Horst Ress, Chief Officer of the German Free Fire Service, Rethwischfeld, at Bad Oldesloe Fire Station during the Service's visit to Germany in June 1990.

The final vehicle line-up at Sproatley Air Park in the spring of 1990. A month later came the announcement of the Air Park's impending closure.

FULL CIRCLE 1991-1993

Despite the disruption caused by the closure of Sproatley Air Park, Humberside Auxiliary Emergency Service succeeded in fulfilling all its operational commitments during the summer of 1990. In the meantime frantic efforts were made to locate suitable alternative premises. Finally, in the autumn, these efforts bore fruit when the Sports & Social Club of J H Fenner invited the Service to share their premises at Marfleet. The location proved ideal for the establishment of personnel, administration and equipment storage facilities, and work commenced immediately on transforming it into a new headquarters.

Simultaneously the Association was invited to garage its vehicles in premises near Leven, on a site to be developed as the new home of Hull Aero club, and this invitation was gratefully accepted.

Despite the logistical problems posed by these widely separated facilities the Service was able to provide valuable assistance to the community during the harsh winter of 1991. Called in by Age Concern, crews worked over several nights to clear ice and snow from the homes of old people, many of whom had been unable to venture out for over a week. In all two complete residential complexes and some twenty individuals were assisted in this way.

Meanwhile work continued on the new headquarters and in January 1991 it was officially opened by the Lord Mayor of Hull in the presence of the County's Chief Emergency Planning Officer and representatives of the German Free Fire Service.

Sadly the opening marked the beginning of a disastrous period for the Service. By midsummer the effects of the recession had forced the sale of the block of buildings in which the new headquarters was located, and it was necessary to vacate the premises, with the paint of its renovation barely dry. The transfer of equipment to the Leven site led to further misfortune. Twice in quick succession the premises there were broken into, and much of the service's equipment, including expensive items such as its portable generator, were stolen.

It says much for the resilience of the organisation that it somehow managed to withstand these demoralising blows and remain operational. In the autumn flying commenced at the Leven site, now licensed and designated Beverley (Lindley) Aerodrome, and in mid-November members of the Service undertook their first standby duty for the Hull Aero Club since the closure of Paull Airfield a decade earlier.

During the course of 1992 members of the Service continued to undertake standby duties at Leven on a regular basis, and worked towards regaining their previous proficiency in aircraft accident work. As a result of training received during this period members gained Red Cross certification in First Aid and Civil Aviation Authority Certification for Firefighting and Rescue Operations to Category 1 Airfield Standard, and by the spring of 1993 Humberside Auxiliary Emergency Service was beginning to recover from the traumas of 1991, and was back in business once more.

On April 2nd 1993 current members of the Service, and those who had served with the Association during its 25 year history, gathered for a reunion. The venue was the Railway Club on Anlaby Rood, scene of the Association's first post- disbandment social a quarter of a century earlier.

EPILOGUE

The world has changed considerably since the disbandment of the Auxiliary Fire Service in 1968. The ending of the Cold War has greatly reduced the risk of the set-piece nuclear attack which gave the post-war AFS its reason for existence, but has brought in its place something almost as menacing. As former Foreign Secretary Douglas Hurd put it: "The world without the Soviet Union is less apocalyptical but in many ways less stable." Additionally incidents ranging from Bhopal to Chernobyl, Lockerbie to Kings Cross have proved that time and technology replace old hazards with new. Ironically the Winter 1992 issue of the Home Office magazine 'Civil Protection' recorded that the period covered by that issue was the worst on record for tragic disasters and concluded by stating that 'the need for emergency planning has never been greater' - while on the opposite page appeared the Home Secretary's statement reducing the level of civil protection and emergency planning...

Writing in the subsequent issue the Association's old friend Eric Alley drew a critical comparison between Britain's threadbare civil protection resources and the systems operated by its European neighbours, observing; "If we look at the rest of the world, and in particular Europe, none of the other nations are so drastically cutting their civil protection systems. The command posts are staying and being modernised; the siren systems have never been allowed to decay in Germany, Sweden, France, Switzerland et al, and are tested regularly. Training continues at all levels and particularly at community level, because that is where the battle for survival, whatever the cause of the disaster, is fought."

For a quarter of a century the Kingston upon Hull AFS Association has sought to operate in keeping with that philosophy, and has worked to fulfil the aims set out in its original constitution. And if its contribution to the well-being of the community has not been as significant as had been hoped at the beginning, it has never been through want of trying.